Journey
of
Hope

THE STORY OF ILAN RAMON, ISRAEL'S FIRST ASTRONAUT

ALAN D. ABBEY

gefen
publishing house בית הוצאה גפן
JERUSALEM ◆ NEW YORK

"Holocaust Helped Define Ramon's Identity," by Elli Wohlgelernter, and the editorials "A Symbolic Mission" and "Tragedy in Space," reprinted with the permission of *The Jerusalem Post*.

"After My Death," by Haim Nachman Bialik,
copyright 2003 by Zmora Bitan-Dvir Publishing House,
English translation of "After My Death" by David P. Stern, copyright 2002.

Astronaut biographies reprinted with the permission of the National Aeronautics and Space Administration (www.nasa.gov).

Photos pages viii, 4,12, 25–27, 48–54, front and back cover, courtesy of NASA.
Photo page 19, Petr Ginz (1928-1944), Moon Landscape, 1942-1944, Pencil on paper
Gift of Otto Ginz, Collection of the Yad Vashem Art Museum.
Photo page 20, courtesy of Joachim Joseph.

Book and cover design by Stephanie and Ruti Design

ISBN 965-229-316-4

3   5   7   9   8   6   4   2

Gefen Publishing House
POB 36004, Jerusalem 91360 Israel
972-2-538-0247
orders@gefenpublishing.com

Gefen Books
12 New Street, Hewlett, NY 11557, USA
516-295-2805
orders@gefenpublishing.com

www.israelbooks.com

Printed in Israel

Send for our free catalogue.

This book is dedicated to the Columbia Seven

Rick Husband, William C. "Willie" McCool,
Michael P. "Mike" Anderson, David M. "Dave" Brown,
Kalpana Chawla, Laurel Clark, and Ilan Ramon,
who lost their lives in the service of their countries
and all humanity.

May their memories be for a blessing.

Acknowledgments

To say that this book appeared in record time is a massive understatement. From conception to completion it was produced in less than three months. It had its beginnings before the liftoff of *Columbia*, it gathered momentum during the flight's triumphant two weeks, and took a radical and unexpected turn in the days after the tragedy that ended the astronauts' lives.

But none of this would have been possible without years of reporting by the writers of *The Jerusalem Post*. Their contributions from 1995 until the present are what made this book possible. Reading their work has been a revelation to me. *The Jerusalem Post* has been on top of this story from the beginning.

My thanks to the many staff writers of *The Jerusalem Post*, past and present, whose work shapes this book. They include Greer Fay Cashman, Gil Hoffman, Herb Keinon, Tovah Lazaroff, Arieh O'Sullivan, David Rudge, Judy Siegel-Itzkovich, Elli Wohlgelemter, and Janine Zacharia.

I would especially like to note the work of Philip Chien, a widely published freelance writer, who contributed daily coverage of Ilan Ramon's flight to the pages of *The Jerusalem Post* earlier this year. Chien's encyclopedic knowledge of NASA's programs, his reporting and his support have been essential to the completion of this project. His review of this manuscript before publication was also invaluable.

Grateful acknowledgment is also made to former President Bill Clinton for the right to reprint his statement about Ilan Ramon.

Thanks are due to *The Jerusalem Post* Publisher Tom Rose, Chief Financial Officer Mark Ziman, Vice Chairman Avi Golan, and Editor-in-Chief Bret Stephens. Their support has helped make this book a reality. I would also like to thank Dror Greenfield and Chava Boylan of Gefen Publishing and Shahar Geva of Tal Shahar. Their support and desire to see this book in print helped make it possible.

In addition, I would like to thank Doreen Ravona and Elaine Moshe of *The Jerusalem Post* Internet and Archives Departments. Without their efforts to track down the articles and pictures, I never would have been able to get started, let alone finish on time. *The Jerusalem Post* Internet update team deserves special credit for its hard work in covering this story as it happened.

Finally, and not least of all, I would like to thank my family—my wife Sheryl, our sons Alex and Ezra, and our daughter Maayan. Their love and encouragement, and their unselfish support of my efforts, which often took me away from them, is deeply appreciated.

Alan D. Abbey
Jerusalem, Israel
April 2003

The tragic loss of seven brave astronauts and the space shuttle Columbia reminds us all of the dangers faced by those who venture into space. That knowledge, however, does little to lessen the shock and ease the sadness we feel at this dark moment. We will return to space because our destiny is to seek out answers that only the exploration of the universe can provide. But we will never forget the sacrifice of those who gave their lives in this bold quest over the years, among them the men and women of Apollo 1, Soyuz 1 and 11, the Challenger, and now, Columbia.

We all pray for the family and friends of the heroes we've lost. My thoughts, too, are with the people of Israel and the family of Colonel Ilan Ramon. It was my honor, as president, to inform Prime Minister Barak in 1999 that an Israeli astronaut would be traveling on board an American shuttle, and I know that Colonel Ramon's mission was a source of great pride for all the people of Israel. The tragedy strikes their hearts deeply, and they share with the American people a tremendous sense of grief. May all who mourn be consoled by our faith in God and in each other.

Bill Clinton
New York, February 2003

Contents

Official crew photo: Seated in front (from left) are astronauts Rick D. Husband , mission commander; Kalpana Chawla, mission specialist; and William C. McCool, pilot. Standing (from left): David M. Brown, Laurel B. Clark, and Michael P. Anderson, all mission specialists; and Ilan Ramon, payload specialist.

Introduction

By Philip Chien

Citizens from more than two dozen countries have flown in space, but only the United States and the former Soviet Union own spacecraft that can carry people. All of those from other countries have flown as guests on American or Russian spacecraft.

Space is international. One shuttle launch in 1997, for example, included space travelers born in five different countries—the United States, France, Russia, the United Kingdom, and Peru. International astronauts fly for a variety of reasons, including politics and science.

The United States initially invited Israel to choose someone to be a passenger with token responsibilities. But Ilan Ramon's talent and the mission he was assigned required him to learn skills more in line with NASA's professional astronauts—and he was up to the challenge.

Whenever an international astronaut flies, especially from a country previously unrepresented in space, there's a lot of interest in the home country. In the United States, for the most part, the shuttle is relegated to a couple of minutes' mention on the news—if that much—unless something about the flight is especially unusual, such as the first female commander or a national hero flying again after three decades.

Because of the terrorist attacks of September 11, 2001, there was much more concern about placing an Israeli on the shuttle. As a precaution, there was unprecedented security for the crew's training and the STS-107 launch, but everything went smoothly.

Ilan Ramon just wanted to fit in as a member of the Columbia's STS-107 crew—and he did. Pilot Willie McCool said, "When somebody comes to a foreign country you'd expect the hosts to embrace the newcomer. In many respects it's been just the opposite. Ilan and [his wife] Rona would have us over on Fridays to celebrate the Israeli tradition of having Friday evening meals together. In a sense, the Ramons embraced the STS-107 crew as much as we've embraced them."

Spaceflight is risky, but so is traveling in a plane or walking across the street. Certainly spaceflight is more dangerous and will continue to be for the foreseeable future. This is something all astronauts understand from the time they fill out their first application. But every astronaut has also decided that the benefits are worth the risks.

Spaceflight veteran Jim Wetherbee said he wanted to give his daughters a sense of how to live their lives if anything bad were to happen to him. "I wanted them to remember two things," he said. "Number one, this is valuable to people on the earth, and I wanted them to realize that I was doing it because of the benefits to humanity. Number two, if I didn't come back, I wanted them to always think about if they had a tough decision to make, think about what would I tell them if I were here, and they would come to the right answer. And that was my way of staying with them."

He said the strain during his spaceflights was greatest for his wife, Robin.

"I think it would be incredibly tough to watch a loved one climb on a rocket," he said. "It's very easy for me to do because I live and die as a consequence of my actions. As Robin explained, it's as alone as you can possibly feel, standing there on the building watching a loved one launch into space. There's nothing anyone can say or do to help you in that kind of situation. So, I feel really fortunate that she's allowed me to do this six times now. I think she's a lot stronger than anybody I've ever met."

Less than one in a thousand Americans knew who Ilan Ramon was before February 1, 2003. The STS-107 flight received even less attention in the United States than most shuttle missions because of its relatively "boring" nature—there was to be no rendezvous, no space walks, no docking with the International Space Station, not even a simple satellite ejection. STS-107 was just a two-week mission dedicated to science—and science in a laboratory isn't supposed to be exciting, at least not to nonscientists.

But that all changed after the loss of the shuttle *Columbia*. In dozens of memorials, people who never met the STS-107 crew talked about how wonderful they had been.

STS-107 was designed to perform more than eighty science experiments, ranging from tests to observe how flames behave in space and understand more about the human body to examinations of dust clouds from space. Fortunately, much of the science on STS-107 was radioed back during the mission. Scientists estimate that as much as 50 to 75 percent of the data can be recovered from many of the experiments, including an experiment performed under the direction of Israeli professor Joachim Joseph, which included the only observation of a dust storm over the Mediterranean Sea. That is the true legacy of the STS-107 mission.

In this book we hope you'll learn a little bit more about Ilan Ramon and that mission.

Hope
Ilan Ramon Takes Off

On the clear, warm morning of Thursday, January 16, 2003, Israel became the twenty-ninth country represented in space when Israeli Air Force Colonel Ilan Ramon along with the rest of the crew of the space shuttle *Columbia*, mission STS-107, rocketed away from Kennedy Space Center at Cape Canaveral, Florida.

Ilan's wife, Rona, their four children, and two family friends watched from NASA's launch control center, about three miles from the launch pad, along with the other astronauts' immediate families. Rona was nervous. Shortly before the event, she commented on how she could not wait for the sixteen-day mission to end. "I don't want to talk about fear," she said. "We're not talking about fear. I'm sure NASA is doing everything that is possible not to take any risk and any chances. The most calm and relaxed person is Ilan."

Those words, perhaps, would come back to haunt Rona Ramon after *Columbia*'s tragic disintegration upon its reentry to the earth's atmosphere two weeks later. Yet the prelaunch moments and the launch itself were festive, patriotic occasions for the hundreds of Israeli dignitaries, Americans, and other guests watching from the viewing stands.

All were smiles at the bon voyage party two nights earlier. "This is definitely exciting, and we're approaching the big moment. It seems like a dream," Rona said at the barbecue. She gave her husband four poems and personal items to take with him. The astronaut's fifteen-year-old son, Assaf, gave his father a note to be opened only in space. According to Jean-Pierre Harrison, husband of crew member Kalpana Chawla, Assaf told people at the party he wanted to be a pilot or astronaut.

Two days later, when the flight was imminent, Harrison said Rona Ramon deserved "a medal, at least, for having all seven members of her party—including children—ready on time" for the launch Thursday morning. After arriving at launch control, all the astronauts' children were sent to a room where they drew a "mission poster" for display on the walls of the facility. Posters extending back into the history of the space program covered the walls. Four bald eagles soared just above eye level as the families peered out from the control center to *Columbia* on its launch pad, three miles away.

While the families watched from their safe perch, Ilan and his six crewmates rode to the launch pad under police escort. A space center worker waved an Israeli

The Columbia takes off from Cape Canaveral, January 16, 2003.

flag as the "astrovan" carrying the astronauts to the pad passed in front of launch control. Despite the large SWAT team on hand to ensure the flight's safety from terrorist attack, the entire shuttle crew looked relaxed. Ilan waved and gave a thumbs-up.

In his personal gear were numerous symbolic items, including a credit card-sized book of Psalms on a microfiche, which he had received from Israel's President Moshe Katsav. He also carried a small kiddush cup with which he planned to mark the onset of the Jewish Sabbath the next evening. His father had given him family photos, and his brother, a letter to read in orbit. Ilan also took along several items symbolic of the Holocaust, including a copy of the pencil drawing *Moon Landscape*, a picture drawn by fourteen-year-old Petr Ginz in 1944 while he was in a Nazi concentration camp.

Ilan explained that the drawing showed how Ginz imagined the earth as viewed from the moon. "Remember, it was long before anybody dreamt about going to the moon. It's kind of a symbolic drawing to symbolize the spirit of this boy. . . . It's related to space, of course, and I feel like I'm taking his vision and his spirit of space." He had chosen the drawing from Israel's Yad Vashem Holocaust Memorial after talking with the memorial's officials.

Ilan also carried a wallet-sized Torah that had been smuggled out of the Bergen-Belsen concentration camp, and a mezuzah wrapped in bits of barbed wire, which had been crafted by an American artist. Ilan was leaving no doubt about how he, the son of a Holocaust survivor, was breaking the confining bonds of the earth and pledging his solidarity with those who never could. In the next few days he would talk several times about how he, the entire Jewish people, and particularly Holocaust survivors and their families, were soaring to the heights after being in the lowest depths just sixty years earlier.

The launch went off smoothly at 10:39 A.M. A few days later, NASA officials noted that a piece of insulating foam had come off the orange external tank and had struck the wing at liftoff. They also reported the loss of tiles off the bottom of the orbiter's left wing, but as of this book's publication, this was only one of the areas under investigation as the cause of the shuttle's disintegration.

The launch began with a loud crack. "Then a roar, followed by vibrations through our feet, as *Columbia* lifted off," Ilan said. As the shuttle cleared the launch tower, Ilan's five-year-old daughter, Noa, said, "I want to see that again!" But in what some later took to be a haunting prophecy, she also said, "I lost my daddy."

Back in Israel, Ilan's father, Eliezer Wolferman, breathed a sigh of relief. "My heart is beating very fast," he said moments after the launch. "This is the moment I was waiting for. I don't have the words to describe it." Now that the launch went well, he said, "perhaps we can all relax."

Columbia streaked into the clear blue sky as white steam trailed behind it at the launch pad.

JOURNEY OF **Hope**

The Idea Is Born

Planning for the flight of *Columbia* with Ilan Ramon aboard began long before the January 16, 2003 launch.

On December 11, 1995, President Bill Clinton and Israeli Prime Minister Shimon Peres announced a plan to conduct joint experiments in space and to train an Israeli astronaut to take part in them. "As part of our effort to support Israel's advances in science and technology, I have today agreed with Prime Minister Peres to proceed with space-based experiments in sustainable water use and environmental protection," the president said at a White House news conference with Peres. "These experiments will take place in unmanned space vehicles, in the shuttle program, and in the International Space Station. And as a part of this effort, we will also train Israeli astronauts to participate in these programs. We look forward to working out the arrangements for this cooperation, and we are absolutely certain that it will benefit Israel's high-tech development as well as our own."

The astronaut was to be a payload specialist for an Israeli scientific experiment to be chosen by the Israeli Space Agency, with the approval of NASA. Later that day, in a background briefing, a senior administration official offered more details of the agreement. "This is a new initiative which builds on discussions that Prime Minister Peres has had with Vice President Gore and others in the area of water resources," the White House press corps was told. "What we've agreed to do is to organize efforts by U.S. and Israeli scientists working together to develop some experiments which can be used aboard our unmanned spacecrafts, aboard the space shuttle, and ultimately, aboard the space station when it is launched and up and running. As part of that, we will be identifying and training Israeli astronauts to participate in the space station program. So this is something that will probably have a fairly long lead time. But the commitment has now been made."

The official's prediction about a long lead time was correct. It would be more than seven years before Ilan would become the first Israeli astronaut. But the story goes back even further than December 1995. It starts with a five-year-old Jerusalem boy—Dean Issacharoff—who innocently raised the issue of putting an Israeli in space to his father, Jeremy Issacharoff, then a political advisor at the Israeli embassy in Washington, D.C. "I went with my dad to the space museum in Washington," Dean said. "I saw pictures of people in space. There was [a picture of] someone from Saudi Arabia [from a previous shuttle flight], and I asked my dad, 'Why isn't there an Israeli astronaut?' He said, 'I don't know.'"

A few days later, as it turned out, Prime Minister Peres was coming to Washington for a meeting with President Clinton. The embassy at the time was looking for nonpolitical issues to bring up with the president. At a preparatory meeting, Issacharoff, remembering his son's question, raised the suggestion of an Israeli astronaut. His boss, Ambassador Itamar Rabinovich, gave him the green light to pursue the idea with the Clinton administration. Issacharoff contacted David Satterfield, an official at the National Security Council, who followed up on the idea.

Dean picks up the tale: "They were trying to figure out how to make the bond closer with America," he explained, "so my dad told someone who brought it up at a planning meeting. They then told Peres, and a week later President Clinton announced there was going to be an Israeli astronaut."

Not everyone in Israel immediately embraced the idea of an Israeli astronaut. As far back as 1984, on a visit to NASA facilities in the United States, Science Minister Yuval Ne'eman, who by 1995 was chairman of the Israel Space Agency (ISA), was invited to propose an Israeli scientific space project that would justify sending an Israeli astronaut on one of NASA's missions. Ne'eman said the idea had been raised among local scientists, but "no one ever came up with a unique idea, project, or product that could be tested only in space and have an important impact on science."

Ne'eman said the ISA—which had a permanent staff of five and functioned under the aegis of Israel's Ministry of Science, Culture, and Sport—did not have funds for training a professional astronaut. "The Japanese paid $300 million—its share of the costs of one man on a mission—to send one of its scientists on a NASA flight. Maybe for us the Americans would charge much less or nothing at all. But we have other things to promote, such as Israel's space-related industries, in which we have much to offer," he said. While the figure Ne'eman gave was an exaggeration (the Spacelab Japan mission [STS-47] cost Japan $50 million for the scientific experiments, plus one payload specialist), his point was that Israel should not send an astronaut to participate in a U.S. space mission unless he or she would be a professional carrying out a special experiment. "We don't need a junket," he said. "It would be embarrassing . . . for an Israeli to go . . . without a unique role in a mission. So far, no Israelis have come up with a unique project that could justify their participation in such a mission."

Most of the Israeli media pounced on the Clinton announcement as a joke. In Knesset corridors, members joked about whether it would be permissible for an

Orthodox astronaut to operate spacecraft controls or take a space walk on the Sabbath, when Jewish law prohibits work. One Knesset member wondered what a Jewish astronaut would do if he found a dinosaur skeleton on a distant planet. Would the Bible have to be reinterpreted or even rewritten? Other Knesset members concocted jokes about a rabbi, a mullah, and a priest in a spaceship.

However, Aby Har-Even, head of the Israel Space Agency, said there would be no shortage of volunteers if the proposal became realistic. "Israelis love challenges," he said at the time. "It would be making history. We don't have a penny in our budget for training astronauts, but if the government decided this was a high priority, we could do it."

Professor Akiva Bar-Nun, ISA director from 1989 to 1994 and a senior Tel Aviv University geophysicist, also saw it in a positive light. "I am now leaning toward the view that sending an Israeli on a NASA mission would be good for the country, not only for the people's morale at minimal financial cost, but also because it would give prominence to Israel and its scientific achievements," he said at the time in a prescient statement.

Many nonprofessional observers have come along on space missions. A Russian space mission in 1987 included a Syrian colonel with no special expertise. NASA took along an American teacher on the space shuttle *Challenger*, which exploded in 1986 soon after takeoff, killing all its crew. Because of that disaster, the era of tourists was over by the time Israel got involved in the American space program. Only professionals, including astronauts from Canada, Japan, Italy, France, Germany, and Spain, were invited and continued to participate in shuttle flights. "They [guest astronauts] must become familiar with all of our procedures, and this will take on the order of a year," said NASA director Daniel Goldin. "The Israelis who will be in space will be required to perform science. We don't carry passengers anymore. They must be scientists."

Who Was Ilan Ramon?

On April 29, 1997, the world knew that a veteran Israeli fighter pilot would join a NASA crew, but it hadn't learned his name. He was identified only as "Colonel A," a forty-two-year-old electrical engineer and F-16 pilot. "Colonel A" had held both command and operational posts in the Israeli Air Force (IAF), including positions in weapons research and development; he had logged many combat missions and had bailed out of his plane at least once in his career. The air force said NASA still had to approve the selection before he was to be sent to the United States for training.

Some in the government were not sure they wanted to send a military pilot. "If it were up to us, we would have put out a tender opening the possibility to travel into space to others—scientists, researchers, engineers," a government spokesman said. But the Israeli Air Force, which was to foot the bill for the pilot's training in the United States, made its preferences clear. The IAF wanted to send one of its pilots into space to mark the state's fiftieth anniversary in 1998. Ilan later said he was selected by the air force because the Israeli Space Agency believed the best person for Israel to send up first would be a military pilot, "exactly as the seven first [*Mercury*] astronauts out of the United States were."

More than a year later, Ilan's name was announced. The IAF never reveals the identities of its pilots, who are usually filmed from behind or with their helmets on. But its hand was forced when NASA unveiled Ilan's name and that of his backup, Lieutenant-Colonel Yitzhak Mayo. Their mission, as originally described, was to test ways to eliminate disturbances in space that affected satellite photographs of the earth. The pair started astronaut training on June 6, 1998.

Was Ilan Ramon the right choice to be Israel's first astronaut? He certainly was an Israeli paradigm: he was a member of Israel's military elite; his mother had survived the Holocaust; his father had fought in Israel's War of Independence; his wife was of Sephardic descent; and his children embodied the blend of Eastern and Western cultures that Israel strives to achieve.

But unlike the caricature of the swaggering, macho pilot, he was modest and unassuming, even shy. In a piece published in *The Jerusalem Post* after Ilan's death, Chuck King, of the International Christian Embassy, wrote of an encounter with a quiet, deferential Ilan at an airport. "Forget every gross generalization you have ever heard about Israelis . . . rude, pushy, demanding, and so on. . . . This one broke the mold. We immediately sensed that we were conversing with someone special, for even though he was soft-spoken, gentle, and unassuming, he also carried with him an air of intelligence, dignity, and charisma." His former commander, retired Colonel Ze'ev Raz, described how Ilan struck him as someone special from the moment of their first encounter. "When I first met him, I immediately noticed his skills and good temper."

Ilan Ramon was born June 20, 1954, in Tel Aviv. He grew up in Beersheva, where his parents still live. He and his wife, Rona, had four children: Assaf, 15, Tal, 13, David, 10, and Noa, 5. Ilan graduated first in his class from Himmelfarb Comprehensive Secondary School in Beersheva in 1972. "He was a wonderful student and such a nice person who always had this terrific smile," said schoolmate Israel German, now director-general of Ben-Gurion University of the Negev. Another of Ilan's former classmates, BGU spokesman Amir Rozenblith, recalled Ilan as the best-looking boy in school. "Not only was he the school 'hunk' who had the prettiest girlfriend, he was also the smartest. Everyone knew he would go far."

After high school, Ilan attended flight-training school as an eighteen-year-old recruit to the pilots' course at Hatzerim air force base outside Beersheva. Beersheva Mayor Ya'acov Terner, who commanded the flight school at the time, spoke of how Ilan showed modesty, intelligence, and goodness of heart even then. "I remember him for those qualities which he carried with him throughout his life," he said.

Long before he received his college degree at thirty-three, Ilan distinguished himself in combat. He flew in the Yom Kippur War in 1973, even though technically he still was a trainee. "I love to fly," Ilan told an interviewer in 2002. "Flying aircraft—fighter aircraft—is great, and I was very happy."

In 1974, Ilan graduated as a fighter pilot from the IAF flight school. For the next two years he was in A-4 Basic Training and Operations. From 1976 to1980 he was in Mirage III-C training and operations programs. In 1980, as part of IAF efforts to establish the first F-16 squadron in Israel, he attended the F-16 training course at Hill Air Force Base in Utah. In the days after his death, Ilan's story so captivated people everywhere that newspapers worldwide went looking for their own links to him. *The Salt Lake City Tribune* made a point of noting the time Ilan had spent in Utah, even though it had occurred more than twenty years earlier.

From 1981 to 1983, Ilan served as a deputy squadron commander of Israel's F-16 squadron. The day after he flew into space in 2003, it was revealed that he had performed an historic mission for Israel during that time. In 1981, Ilan was one of eight Israeli F-16 pilots who destroyed the Iraqi Osirak nuclear reactor near Baghdad in a lightning raid that shocked the world. The mission was a milestone in Israeli aviation history because the planes flew over enemy Arab territory for hours without being detected. The pilots flew in a tightly bunched formation to send off a radar signal resembling that of a large commercial airliner. Although the move was widely condemned at the time, analysts later concluded that it set back an Iraqi nuclear weapons program and eased U.S. operations in the Persian Gulf War of 1991.

Raz, commander of the 1981 mission, said Ilan was the first officer he informed about the order to bomb the reactor. Ramon first thought the round-trip would be too far to go on a single planeload of fuel. "He went back to his desk with his maps, and after a few hours he entered my office and said, 'Sorry, but it's slightly out of range,'" Raz recalled. But the inherent danger of the mission did not prevent Ilan, who at twenty-seven was the youngest member of the F-16 squadron, from volunteering for the most dangerous rear position. Ilan selected the attack route, and navigated and planned fuel consumption for the four-hour round-trip over hostile territory. Major General Amos Yadlin, one of the mission's pilots, told Reuters there was no option for refueling in midflight. "Logistically, he achieved what was thought impossible," Yadlin said. "Ilan was only a captain, but we knew he was the right choice for the job. He was cool-headed, modest, sort of a humble hero—not like most macho top-gun flyers."

The following year Ilan flew missions over Lebanon as part of Operation Peace for Galilee. From 1983 to 1987, he attended Tel Aviv University, where he received a Bachelor of Science degree in electronics and computer engineering. From 1988 through 1992, he rose through the ranks and ended up as commander of Israel's F-16 Squadron. He had recorded a total of one thousand flight hours in his F-16 by then, and an additional three thousand flight hours on A-4, Mirage III-C, and F-4 planes. In 1994, Ilan reached the rank of colonel and took control of the air force's weapons development and acquisitions department. When asked why Ilan was not promoted to the rank of general, Yadlin said that Ilan was too nice. "To reach this, you need to be pushy," he said.

By 1997, nearly two years after President Clinton had made the announcement about having an Israeli fly on an American shuttle, Ilan was considering retirement. Then late one afternoon, just before he was to leave his office, a colleague called and asked if he'd like to become an astronaut. At first, Ilan thought the offer was a joke.

"I told him, 'Come on, I don't have time for jokes now,'" Ilan said. "When I was a kid growing up, nobody in Israel ever dreamed—well most people wouldn't

Ilan, photographed in the rear station of the T-38 trainer jet, prepares for a flight from Ellington Field near Johnson Space Center.

dream—of being an astronaut because it wasn't on the agenda. So I never thought I would have been an astronaut. When I was selected, I really jumped almost to space. I was very excited." Yadlin said Ilan was one of three candidates considered by the IAF, but the choice was unanimous.

In 1998, Ilan reported for training at Johnson Space Center in Houston. He relocated to Houston along with his wife, Rona, and their children. The Ramons made themselves at home in Houston. While in training, Ilan and his family attended Congregation Shaar Hashalom near Johnson Space Center. Maya Grijalva, a family friend, told the *Houston Chronicle* how Ilan and his family became part of the community. "We'd been to his house. He'd been to our houses," she said. "He was a great man, but a very down-to-earth person. He made himself one of the crowd. He always talked to the kids. He always played with the kids. He was that kind of person."

As the flight neared, press and public attention ratcheted upwards. Ilan began making public appearances and giving interviews. In his appearances, he regularly divulged personal details, in addition to talking about the flight. The mix of the two added to the drama and the interest in him. Ilan said he would carry with him various artifacts that "emphasize the unity of the people of Israel and the Jewish communities abroad." Ilan did not reveal at first what those would be, but he told Jewish groups in the United States that he saw his planned mission in space as a "good stage to proclaim that we [in Israel] need you, and you [in the Diaspora] need us."

He began identifying himself as the son of a father who was a refugee from Germany and who had fought in Israel's War of Independence and of a mother who had survived Auschwitz. Being his country's first astronaut, Ilan said, was part of a "miracle" that stretched back fifty years. His connection to the Holocaust was an important factor in his life long before his flight into space. Yadlin spoke of how Ilan told him about his parents' past while they were preparing for the Iraq mission in 1981. "If I can prevent a second Holocaust, I'm ready to sacrifice my life for this," Yadlin quoted Ilan as saying at the time.

Ilan was not an observant Jew, but he said early on that while on board the shuttle he wanted to eat kosher food and to try to mark the Jewish *Sabbath*. There had been other Jewish astronauts, most notably David Wolf, who flew on the shuttle *Endeavour*, and Judith Resnik, who died in the *Challenger* explosion in 1986. However, Ilan was the first to request kosher meals. "This is symbolic," he said. "I thought it would be nice to represent all kinds of Jews, including religious ones." He joked about affixing a mezuzah to the shuttle's door, but said it was up to the commander.

Ilan said his being Israeli did not cause any problems inside NASA. "Among the astronauts I blend in pretty well," he said. "Sometimes, of course, they talk about Israel's security problems, and that's natural. Most of the time I'm just another astronaut having fun. Nothing special." Ramon said he was amazed to walk in the corridors of NASA and see astronauts from so many nations. "I was sure I was not in the U.S.," he said. "I was even more amazed to hear American astronauts speaking Russian, and French, and Japanese."

Ramon was planning to spend one final month after the flight in Houston in debriefing and post-experiment follow-up. He then intended to return to Israel with his family to a new home in Ramat Gan.

Training and Waiting

By late 1999, plans were set for a 2001 launch for Ilan's flight, but few details about the mission were available. In 2000, *Air Force Magazine* revealed that Ilan was to be a crew member on *Columbia*, flight STS-107, then scheduled for launch in April or May 2001. NASA officially announced Ilan's participation in the crew, along with astronauts Mike Anderson, Kalpana Chawla, Dave Brown, and Laurel Clark, in September 2000. In December, NASA added Rick Husband and Willie McCool.

On a visit to Israel, NASA Administrator Daniel Goldin said Ilan would be launched into space May 23, 2002, instead of mid-2001 as had been originally intended.

The shuttle's orbit and launch window would be tailored to fit the science requirements for the Israeli-sponsored MEIDEX (Mediterranean Israeli Dust Experiment) project. The experiment was designed to test how dust particles from storms affect the climate of the Middle East. MEIDEX featured a specially calibrated video camera that would take images of the earth through six filters. The astronauts would look for dust and aim the camera. Meanwhile, scientists on the ground would fly aircraft through the dust storms to make additional measurements. NASA atmospheric scientist Jack Kaye said the data was expected to be valuable, and it wasn't something NASA would have done on its own, because of the intense effort required.

The decision to fly Ilan Ramon on the mission also meant a fundamental change in his activities as a crew member. Normally a guest astronaut—a "payload specialist" in NASA's vernacular—flies only to conduct a specific set of science experiments or to fill a role that can't be filled by a career NASA astronaut. A large percentage of payload specialists have been international astronauts, such as the Canadians that NASA has an agreement to fly each year.

Obviously no NASA astronaut could fill the political role of being an Israeli citizen, even though most could have been trained to operate MEIDEX. The MEIDEX experiment would only occupy Ilan during the portion of the day when the shuttle was flying over the Mediterranean Sea or the second area of interest over the eastern Atlantic Ocean. It would be absurd to have him aboard simply to conduct the MEIDEX experiment. So NASA and the Israeli Space Agency gave Ilan a promotion of sorts and made him a full payload crew member like the career

NASA astronauts who would be assigned later. Ilan would learn how to operate many of the payloads and take a full workload like the other mission specialists. As a non-career astronaut Ilan wouldn't have any shuttle responsibilities, such as opening or closing the payload bay doors or going for emergency space-walk training.

Ilan was given mission specialist astronaut training along with the 1998 astronaut class and acquired the additional skills he would need to fulfill his role. "He's working as many payloads as anybody else on the flight," said Commander Rick Husband, who became a close friend of Ilan. "He's gone through a significant amount of training. I would say he's probably one of the best-trained payload specialists we've ever flown. Ilan is fully integrated into every aspect of the mission. He is not an observer; he's a full member of the crew in every way."

In June 2002, with yet more deadlines come and gone, NASA again delayed the flight. The shuttle, set for takeoff on July 19, was suspended because of small cracks found on part of the main propulsion systems on all four space shuttle vehicles: *Atlantis*, *Columbia*, *Discovery*, and *Endeavour*. The flight was to be delayed at least a few weeks to give NASA managers time to better understand the cracks. Then, when two International Space Station missions were given higher priority, the *Columbia* mission was pushed back in line, first to November, then December, and finally January. The technical problems, management decisions, and higher priority flights resulted in eighteen delays.

Ilan said everyone in the crew was eagerly awaiting the launch. "I'm sure everybody's excited to go—at least myself and my family," he said. "My family has had to sacrifice a lot. I have a lot of patience, and to be with these magnificent crew members is a pleasure. I don't want to be delayed again, but I'm sure we'll have a wonderful time together, as we have in the last two and a half years of training."

In December 2002, Ilan and the crew of STS-107 finally completed their dress rehearsal. It included a practice countdown with the launch team, inspections of the shuttle and the equipment the astronauts were to use in space, checks of the orange launch and entry suits the crew would wear, and lessons in how to drive the M-113 armored personnel carrier. The M-113 was stationed at the base of the launch pad for the launch. If a major emergency occurred at launch, the astronauts were to exit the shuttle and jump into wire baskets that would whisk them to the base of the launch pad. There they would enter a bomb shelter or get into the M-113 and drive as far away from the pad as quickly as possible. The irony, of course, was that the astronauts had no training or escape route for the disaster that would eventually overtake them.

In contrast to his intense training, the final days before the launch were a restful time for Ilan and his crewmates. A week before takeoff, they went into isolation and only came in contact with people who had been medically cleared. They were allowed to see their spouses.

On January 13, 2003, Ilan and his six crewmates flew to Kennedy Space Center. "I'm happy to be here, finally," Ilan said after his arrival. "It was a pleasure to go the long way—two and a half years—because of the great team, great crew, great trainers, great flight directors, great engineers. The route to the target is more important than the target. We're going to go for the target, but we enjoy the route as well."

There were many news reports of tight security surrounding Kennedy Space Center because of the heightened fears of terrorism ascribed to the presence of an Israeli astronaut. NASA attempted to play them down. Shuttle Test Director Jeff Spaulding said he had not noticed any unusual security precautions. "The average person coming to work each day probably won't even notice most of the stuff."

Nonetheless, as a post-September 11 security measure, NASA did not announce the actual launch window until the day before liftoff. In addition, security around Ilan was tight to prevent terror attacks. Before he went into medical quarantine, he was protected by two police officers at dinner in restaurants. "It's not something he's used to," said Aby Har-Even. "We were quite surprised at the very strict security."

Ilan said he hoped the mission would provide Israelis with a cheerful distraction from the political conflict in Israel at the time. "I think [Israelis] are very happy to be distracted by my flight and NASA flights, maybe to forget a little bit of their problems and get out there with us," he said. Ilan also used his platform to speak of the need for universal cooperation, a common theme among astronauts, who, from space, see the earth in its entirety.

"There's no better place to emphasize the unity of people in the world than flying to space," he said. "It goes the same for any country, Arab country, whatever—we are all the same people, we are all human beings and I believe that most of us, almost all of us, are good people."

A few days before the liftoff, NASA gave the final clearance for the shuttle despite finding a small crack on a stainless steel ball used in the rocket's fuel lines on another shuttle. The ball was designed to permit propellant lines to vibrate without breaking during launch. NASA put a test ball through stresses equivalent to 140 shuttle flights to assure that the mission would not be harmed even if one of the balls on *Columbia* were damaged during launch.

About three hundred Israelis flew to Florida to watch the takeoff, most of them guests of Ilan and the Israel Space Agency. Excellent weather was forecast. The crew took a final training flight in NASA high-performance aircraft.

Prime Minister Ariel Sharon spoke to Ilan the day before the flight. In a speech to supporters of the Weizmann Institute, Israel's science university, he told them about his conversation with the astronaut. "I was excited, the Minister of Education was excited, and I believe that the pilot was the most excited," Sharon said. "We had a long talk, and I can tell you that Colonel Ramon is a man bursting with national pride. Colonel Ramon's flight and his mission into space are a source of honor to us all, and his success is yet another step in Israel's integration into the space age. We wish him and the entire crew of the *Columbia* space shuttle success in their mission and a safe return home."

In their conversation, Ilan said it was a great privilege to represent Israel. "I'm going to carry special things and try to express something about the unity of the Israeli people and the Jewish community," he told Sharon. "I have some ideas, but for the time being, I will keep them deep inside of me. It will be a surprise." As he had been telling others with increasing frequency, Ilan described to Sharon the significance of a son of a Holocaust survivor going into space. "I know my flight is very symbolic for the people of Israel, especially the survivors, the Holocaust survivors," Ilan said. "Because I was born in Israel, many people will see this as a dream come true."

The Jerusalem Post, February 4, 2003

Holocaust Helped Define Ramon's Identity
By Elli Wohlgelernter

Being the son of an Auschwitz survivor was a defining part of astronaut Ilan Ramon's identity and the reason he chose to take with him to space something from that period.

Avner Shalev, chairman of the Yad Vashem directorate, said Ramon approached the Israeli Holocaust memorial center.

"He approached us, because it was so central to his identity; not only the remembrance, but a very central part of his being, as a human being, as an Israeli," Shalev said. "He was born here, he was a pilot, and the image of the mighty Israeli—the sabra—was part of him. Nevertheless, another part, a very central one, was the remembrance of the *Shoah*, as continuity to Jewish life and continuity to his own family."

Ramon expressed that identity, Shalev said, by taking not just one symbol of that era, but three: a miniature Torah scroll that, along with its owner, survived the Bergen-Belsen concentration camp; a small pencil drawing, titled "*Moon Landscape*," created by a 14-year-old Jewish boy during his incarceration in the Theresienstadt ghetto; and a *mezuzah* ringed with bits of barbed wire, symbolizing the spiritual resistance within the confining perimeters of Nazi concentration camps and ghettos.

Joachim Joseph, 71, an atmospheric physicist at Tel Aviv University who oversaw an Israeli experiment aboard the shuttle, and who is a survivor of Bergen-Belsen, lent the miniature Torah scroll that Ramon carried with him to space.

Joseph was given the miniature Torah by an Amsterdam rabbi who shared his barracks in 1944. Joseph had just turned 13, and the rabbi secretly arranged a bar mitzvah ceremony at 4 a.m. in the prisoners' barracks.

"'After the ceremony,' he said, 'you take this, this scroll that you just read from, because I will not leave here alive. But you must promise me that if you get out, you'll tell the story,'" Joseph said.

The rabbi was killed two months later, and Joseph was freed from the camp in a prisoner exchange in 1945, one month before it was liberated by the Americans and British.

While at Joseph's home two years ago to discuss the space experiments, Ramon noticed the scroll and asked if he could take it, along with a journal of Joseph's, on the flight.

"He was deeply affected," Joseph said. "He almost cried. I feel now that I finally was able to fulfill my promise to Rabbi Dasberg 50 years ago."

While in space, Ramon showed the Torah scroll to Prime Minister Ariel Sharon during a televised conference.

"This represents more than anything the ability of the Jewish people to survive despite everything during horrible periods," Ramon told Sharon.

The *mezuzah* Ramon took with him into space had a silver-and-copper Star of David ringed with bits of barbed wire, a gift from San Francisco artist Aimee Golant, whose grandparents survived the Holocaust.

While training to become an astronaut, Ramon approached the 1939 Club of Los Angeles—whose members are Holocaust survivors—and expressed his desire to take a *mezuzah* into space, said

Golant, whose grand-parents also belong to the 1939 Club.

Ramon wanted no publicity about his special "space" *mezuzah*, Golant said. "He told me, 'The people who need to know about it, will know.'"

Shalev said the pencil drawing Ramon took to space was not the original, contrary to various media reports.

"It was a copy—we wouldn't dare send the original, because they are so rare and unique for us," Shalev said. "Even NASA regulations forbid it. So they gave us instructions

Petr Ginz's Moon Landscape

exactly how to make and prepare the replica, and we did it. We also had a photograph of [the artist] Petr Ginz, which was sent with it, and Ilan took both of them."

Ramon had spoken of Ginz's science-fiction drawing while he was training at the Houston Space Center.

"I feel that my journey fulfills the dream of Petr Ginz 58 years on," Ramon said. "A dream that is ultimate proof of the greatness of the soul of a boy imprisoned within the ghetto walls, the walls of which could not conquer his spirit. Ginz's drawings, stored at Yad Vashem, are a testimony to the triumph of the spirit."

Yehudit Shendar, Yad Vashem's senior curator, had found the drawing about four months ago while searching for something appropriate for Ramon to take with him.

"I suggested that this should be the item that Ilan take to the space shuttle," Shendar said yesterday from Boston. "I think it was quite an easy choice —realizing that Ilan was going on a shuttle space

The Torah scroll that Ilan took with him into space.

flight, it was easy to connect between him and between Petr and the Jewish state. Looking from the moon to the earth—I found it incredible that a young boy of 14 could envision the site that Ilan himself was about to see on his trip."

Ginz was deported to Auschwitz from Theresienstadt on September 28, 1944, and was immediately gassed upon arrival at Birkenau the next day. Ramon's mother, now 75, and his grandmother were liberated from Auschwitz on January 27, 1945.

"I know my flight is very symbolic for the people of Israel, especially the survivors, the Holocaust survivors," Ramon said once in the months leading up to his space mission. "Because I was born in Israel, many people will see this as a dream come true. I'm kind of the proof for my parents and their generation that whatever we've been fighting for in the last century is becoming true."

The Flight

Ilan Ramon was a veteran of thousands of hours of flight in supersonic fighter jets, but he found *Columbia*'s takeoff a whole new experience. "The launch was pretty exciting, a lot of noise, shaking," he later told earthbound interviewers from space. Like the cool fighter pilot he was, he adjusted quickly. "After a minute or so I got used to it, and it went pretty smoothly," he said in the laconic tones used by pilots around the world.

Daniel Ayalon, the Israeli ambassador to the United States, was moved as he watched the takeoff. "I was thinking the skies were colored blue and white—our national colors," he said. "We had deep, beautiful blue skies with this smoke [from the rocket boosters] coming out. In two generations, we're moving from the lowest ebb . . . the darkest point of our history, to a very great moment of excellence and achievement."

In Israel, the country came to a near standstill for the moment. Virtually every television in the country was tuned in to the launch, which was broadcast live on television and radio.

All appeared normal at launch. The boosters separated at the scheduled two-minute mark and opened their parachutes for splashdown in the ocean. *Columbia*'s three engines burned one thousand gallons of fuel a second. Eight and a half minutes into the flight, the loudspeakers rang out with "MECO" (main engine cutoff). Once *Columbia* settled safely in orbit, mission control radioed up, "A big welcome to Ilan as you join the international community of human space flight."

The period after launch was a busy one. Ilan, Payload Commander Mike Anderson, and Mission Specialist Laurel Clark reconfigured the crew cabin. They folded and stored the chairs used for launch and landing and stored their bright orange launch and entry suits. They then spent two hours activating the Spacehab module, in which most of the experiments were to be performed.

Ilan and the other astronauts then got down to the mundane routines of living in space. For his first meal Ilan selected chicken and noodles, green beans with mushrooms, crackers, strawberries, trail mix, brownies, and orange juice. His kosher chicken dish—which he had specifically requested—was not a freeze-dried "astronaut package," but had come out of a supermarket. He heated it in a microwave oven and wolfed it down.

After the meal, half of the crew—Pilot Willie McCool, Anderson, and Mission

Specialist Dave Brown—went to sleep. Ilan, Husband, Clark and Mission Specialist Kalpana Chawla continued to organize the shuttle for its two weeks in space.

Ilan set up a notebook computer for use with the MEIDEX project, sponsored by the Israel Space Agency and controlled from the ground in Houston by Joachim Joseph of Tel Aviv University. Joseph, himself a Holocaust survivor, had given Ilan the miniature Torah scroll. While planning the experiment together, the two became good friends. Ilan used the computer to send commands to move cameras that measured desert dust in the atmosphere to gauge its effect on climate change. The computer also controlled the experiment's video recorders.

Then Ilan started another project that would study the effects of space on the human body. Next, he set up equipment used for blood collections. He spit out a sample of saliva, which was placed into a twenty-eight-liter freezer. By the mission's end, the freezer was to be filled with samples of the crew's saliva, blood, and urine, as part of continuing tests of spaceflight's impact on human beings.

Finally, after a long day, Ilan prepared for sleep. The astronauts who had gone to sleep after launch were awakened, and those in Ilan's shift briefed them on what they had accomplished. Ilan climbed into his sleeping bunk at 4:39 A.M. Israel time, on Friday, January 17.

Ilan's first opportunity to view Israel from space was disappointing, however, he said the next day. "It went too fast. It was mostly cloudy, so I couldn't see much of Israel," he said. "But of course I was excited." Later in the flight, in a conversation with Prime Minister Ariel Sharon, he described a clearer view of Israel.

Excited was certainly a word that could be used to describe how people in Israel were feeling. "An Israeli in Space" screamed the headline in *Yediot Aharonot,* the nation's largest newspaper. It ran a full-page photo of the astronaut showing the Israeli flag sewn onto his space suit.

"One giant leap for Israel," the newspaper said, paraphrasing Neil Armstrong's famous words. "One of ours is in space. Ilan's launch into space today is perhaps a tiny, insignificant event in the development of our scientific infrastructure, but certainly it is an outstanding and significant milestone on this endless road." *Ma'ariv's* headline was no less enthusiastic. "He Touches the Skies," the Hebrew daily said. *Ma'ariv* described the flight as "a decisive step in Israel's participation in space research, which is essential for its technological progress and its security."

Throughout the flight, news coverage was intensive, and, for the most part, positive. During the two and a half weeks of *Columbia's* sojourn in space, most mainstream commentators in Israel were respectful, if not awestruck, by the flight and by Ilan himself. His charm and winning smile disarmed almost all.

Editorial, *The Jerusalem Post,* January 17, 2003

A Symbolic Mission

"For Israel and for the Jewish community, it's something beyond being in space, it's a very symbolic mission." So said IAF Colonel Ilan Ramon, summing up the importance of his mission as Israel's first astronaut aboard the US space shuttle *"Columbia."*

Ramon couldn't have been more right, and the symbolism of his mission came just when we needed it most.

The U.S. decided to invite Israel to attach an astronaut to the space shuttle back in 1991 during the heady days of the Clinton administration. Those were different times.

The stock market was soaring, hi-tech and dot coms were the new messiahs. New immigrants were streaming in. Syria was three years away from turning down peace, Arafat was three and a half years from going to war. The future seemed boundless and filled with hope and excitement. So when Binyamin Netanyahu announced that one of ours would be looking down at us from space, we filed the good news away with the rest of the good news and moved on, feeling very good as usual.

But since September 2000 our mood has changed. The markets are way down, as is immigration. We are fighting boycotts and threats of boycotts in Europe and threats of divestment on U.S. university campuses. Anti-Semitism worldwide is at a peak unseen since the 1930s. And of course there is the war. There are 768 fewer of us today than there were in 1997.

So yes, the mood has changed. We are depressed and often hopeless. Our leaders, particularly now before elections, spend too much time spreading around blame for our problems and too little time addressing them.

But here comes Ramon in a space suit and tells us that there is no horizon too distant to cross and no height too high for us to reach. We Israelis can go anywhere. When we set our mind to it, he reminds us, we can make the desert bloom and build modern cities on sand dunes. And we can reach for the stars.

Ilan and his crewmates spent their first days on the shuttle adjusting to the environment. In fact, the work on the flight absorbed him so that he didn't pause to take a break for the Sabbath, just one day after his takeoff. "We have been so busy that I forgot to think about the Sabbath," Ilan said the following day in the astronauts' first broadcast from space. "Well, I am secular, and I am here with a special team and roommates, and I am busy just like they are. The only thing I did have is a kiddush cup, and hopefully, I will be able to do it next Friday."

He called the mission "a great start" and described it as an opening for "great science from Israel, and, hopefully, for our neighbors in the Middle East." Ilan knew he wasn't the first Middle Easterner to fly in a shuttle, but he attempted to speak of the universality of the experience and its ability to draw people together. "I feel like I represent the State of Israel and the Jews, but I represent also all our neighbors, and I hope it contributes to the whole world," he said.

In his daily experiments, Ilan lit tiny fires in a sealed container. The flames were kept small, were triple-contained, and used a minute amount of fuel. In space, flames burn much more slowly than on earth, permitting scientists to examine the combustion process in great detail. The fires were part of the Laminar Soot Process Experiment, which looked at how soot is generated. The experiment was carried out on the shuttle in 1997, and its experimenters were flying it again to glean additional data. Some flames create more soot than others, and reducing soot minimizes pollution. Scientists hoped that by understanding how soot forms, they could make cleaner burning engines which would reduce exhaust. Ilan spoke with payload control while adjusting dozens of settings to achieve the best possible performance from the experiment. After the experiment's first run was completed, mission control radioed back. "Thanks for the hard work," they said. "The LSP science guys have been looking at the data and are extremely happy with what they've seen."

"It's only because of the hard work by the training team," Ilan answered.

Ilan conducted an additional thirteen runs of the soot experiment, plus two other flame experiments—one on tiny balls of flames that hang in midair until they burn themselves out, and another on how spraying water in a mist can put out fire. One of the experiments Ilan watched over was a "chemical garden" developed by students from ORT Kiryat Motzkin School in Haifa, which involved growing blue cobalt crystals and white calcium crystals, the colors of the Israeli flag.

As the flight continued, engineers at mission control attempted to solve a mundane but annoying problem: water removal in the Spacehab module. Each astronaut was generating water, primarily humid breath and evaporated sweat. The

Ilan floats in a small life raft during an emergency egress training session in the Neutral Buoyancy Laboratory near the Johnson Space Center.

shuttle had a system for removing the excess water and dumping it overboard. In addition, Spacehab, the canister where the experiments were being performed, had water removal capabilities. The problem was with a spinning separator that used centrifugal force to separate the water from the air. Mission control asked the astronauts to shut off a malfunctioning system after electrical spikes were noticed in an electronics box close to the leaks. About two liters of water had leaked. The crew found an extremely low-tech solution to the problem: they used towels to mop it up.

The next day, Ilan took a break from his nonstop work. NASA's flight rules call for space travelers to take two half days off on longer shuttle flights. During their leisure time, astronauts often talk to their families, send e-mail to friends, and spend time looking out at the earth. One of Ilan's official tasks that day, however, was to take a telephone call from Israeli Prime Minister Sharon. The call was aired live on Israeli television and radio. Some dismissed the call as a campaign ploy by Sharon, who was facing a general election in less than a week, but it is routine for NASA to offer a VIP phone call whenever an international astronaut flies. Sharon and Education Minister Limor Livnat conducted the conversation as a carefully selected and photogenic audience of students and others watched.

Rick Husband (left) and Ilan are pictured in the Spacehab Research Double Module above the Columbia.

Ilan used the occasion to emphasize two issues he had raised consistently: Israel's beauty and specialness and the rise of the Jewish people from the ashes of the Holocaust. As he spoke to Sharon, Ilan displayed a wallet-sized Torah scroll and told how it was saved from the Bergen-Belsen concentration camp. He said it symbolized "more than anything, the ability of the Jewish people to survive everything, including horrible periods, and go from the darkest days to days of hope and faith in the future." Ilan briefly told the story of the scroll, which at one point floated out of his hand.

"It is a small Torah scroll that sixty years ago a little boy in Bergen-Belsen received from the rabbi of Amsterdam. The rabbi taught him from it for his bar mitzvah. That thirteen-year-old boy read the weekly portion from this Torah. . . . That boy, Joachim Joseph, survived the Holocaust, arrived in Israel, fought in the country's wars, and then went on to become a distinguished professor of planetary physics. I am moved to hold this."

Ilan's talk with Sharon took place just a few days prior to the Jewish holiday of Tu B'Shvat, which marks the beginning of the spring in Israel. Not one to miss a symbolic moment, Ilan, whose first name means "tree" in Hebrew, called on people to plant millions of trees in the next year to honor Israel and improve its environment. He also tried to raise the spirits of people in Israel. "I think that the people of Israel, and the Jewish people as a whole, are a marvelous people," he said, aware of his nation's eyes on him. "From space, Israel looks like it does on a map, small but charming. I think we have a great people in Israel, and we have to maintain our Jewish heritage. I think it is very, very important to preserve our historical tradition, and I mean historical and religious traditions."

Sharon, not known for great displays of emotion, was clearly moved. "I would like to congratulate you for standing up as a Jew," he said. "Like you, I believe we are a special nation that has faced many difficulties and can achieve great things. You are one of our best achievements. What do you see from there that we don't see from here?"

"We see the earth, which is beautiful," the astronaut said.

Ilan was flanked during the twenty-minute conversation by three of his crewmates—Rick Husband, Kalpana Chawla, and Laurel Clark. They smiled politely throughout the Hebrew conversation, and responded to Sharon's one comment in English. The prime minister invited them to visit Israel, and particularly to see Jerusalem, which Sharon called the "eternal capital of Israel," a statement some saw as a political thrust. Husband accepted the invitation on behalf of the crew.

Among the guests invited to the prime minister's office to watch the conversation were four ninth-grade students from a Jerusalem high school. Itai Simhoni asked Ilan what his most significant and unexpected experience had been so far. The most moving experience, apart from looking out the window, was that of floating, Ilan said. "You don't see us float now because we have to stay in front of the camera, but the floating—going to sleep in a little closet and floating inside it—is something like the magicians show us. It really is tremendous." Asked what it felt like to be in outer space, Ilan replied, "I feel right at home."

While these pleasant conversations were being held with the spacecraft crew, concerns were quietly being expressed on earth about possible damage to *Columbia* during takeoff. NASA contractor Boeing was being pressed to assess the damage apparently caused by the foam insulation that had fallen from *Columbia*'s external fuel tank during liftoff. On January 23, Boeing officials wrote that the spacecraft would likely make a safe return even if the foam insulation had caused "significant tile damage." Boeing

Ilan wears his training version of the full-pressure launch and entry suit prior to a training session in the Space Vehicle Mockup Facility at the Johnson Space Center.

assumed the foam debris had struck part of *Columbia*'s left wing, including its toughened leading edge and thermal tiles covering the landing gear, the *Houston Chronicle* reported.

Boeing concluded that the shuttle had a "safe return capability," although it cautioned about some of the assumptions its engineers used in their predictions. One expert wrote, "*Columbia*'s flight condition is significantly outside of test database," because engineers were relying on scientific models involving impacts from chunks of foam three cubic inches in size, according to a *Chronicle* report ten days after the accident. Officials believe the foam that struck *Columbia* measured 1,920 cubic inches. Four days after the first Boeing report, NASA officials at Johnson Space Center in Houston called experts at Boeing's Langley research facility in Hampton, Virginia, to ask what might happen if the shuttle's tires were not inflated when it attempted to land, the *Chronicle* reported. A Boeing executive told the newspaper that kind of follow-up question wasn't unusual.

The *Chronicle* quoted Michael I. Mott, Boeing vice president and general manager of NASA systems, as saying: "Many times we generate a report and it generates a question somebody else notices. These are ongoing things, and we never give up and declare victory and move on. They are continuously reviewed to make sure we haven't missed something." NASA spokesman Keith Henry told the Houston paper that an engineer from Langley responded that excessive heating due to failure of the shuttle's thermal protection system could cause damage to *Columbia*'s wheels and tires, which could prevent pilots from lowering the gear at landing. Officials at Johnson acknowledged that was an important concern, Henry said. Still, Boeing was standing by its initial assessment.

"There was a very rigorous process applied involving some of the top technical talent on this planet," Mott told the Houston paper. "We thought we were going to bring *Columbia* safely home. We believed that then, we believe that now. We think that analysis was right on."

The night before the accident was the beginning of Ilan's third Sabbath in space. He had said two days earlier that he had not had an opportunity to celebrate the Sabbath in the previous two weeks because of the mission's busy schedule, but that he would do so on the night before landing. No one will ever know if he did.

A Tragic Return

Toward the end of the *Columbia* flight, both Israel and NASA shifted their attention briefly to other matters. A few days before the planned landing, NASA observed the anniversary of its two space tragedies: the *Challenger* explosion of January 28, 1986 and the *Apollo* spacecraft fire that killed three on January 27, 1967. In Israel, the country turned its attention to its general elections. On January 28, five days before the expected touchdown, Prime Minister Sharon's Likud party won a smashing victory. Later that day, President Bush gave his widely anticipated 2003 State of the Union speech in which he continued to build the case for disarming Iraq.

At the end of that week, however, anticipation was building for the *Columbia*'s return. By Saturday, February 1, *Columbia* had completed 255 orbits on its sixteen-day mission and had begun the hour-long descent from orbit toward the landing strip. During that time its engines were off, and, as with other shuttle landings, the ship essentially became a glider. Its 20,000 thermal tiles protected against temperatures as high as 3,000 degrees centigrade.

The first signs of trouble came just before 9 A.M., about twenty minutes before the shuttle was scheduled to land. *Columbia* was descending over the western United States. There was an unusual heat buildup of thirty degrees inside the left wheel well. Investigators later said they believe the tire inside didn't deflate. Reentry heat burned through the wires to the sensors and caused the loss of readings.

Jeff Kling, mission control officer for maintenance, mechanical arm, and crew systems, noticed something wrong and was the first to report a problem. In tapes released by NASA in the days following the disaster, Kling can be heard saying, "FYI, I've just lost four separate temperature transducers on the left side of the vehicle—hydraulic return temperatures, two of them on system one and one each on systems two and three."

Flight Director Leroy Cain responded: "Is there anything common to them . . . or anything? I mean, you're telling me you lost 'em all at the same time?"

Kling: "No, not exactly. They were within probably four or five seconds of each other."

The flight controllers, experienced in this sort of work, did not panic or change their tone of voice. Did they realize something was wrong? Controllers initially seemed to think they had just lost some sensors, which is not a major problem. Then something else happened.

Kling noticed, "We just lost tire pressure on left outboard, left inboard, both tires."

Astronaut Charlie Hobaugh, sitting in mission control, acknowledged the crew receiving a warning on the shuttle.

Hobaugh: "*Columbia?* Houston. We see your tire pressure messages and we did not copy your last."

Shuttle Commander Rick Husband responded, "Roger, uh, but . . . "

While those turned out to be Husband's last recorded words, the loss of communication was initially not a concern. It is common to lose communication with spacecraft upon its reentry into the earth's atmosphere. But the gap became worrisome, and it marked the beginning of the drama that was to unfold.

Cain: "There's no commonality between all these tire pressure instrumentations and the hydraulic pressure instrumentations?"

Kling: "Uh, no sir. We've also lost the nose gear down talk-back and the right main gear down talk-back."

More failure reports came in. Houston tried to reach *Columbia* by simple UHF radio.

Hobaugh: "*Columbia?* Houston. UHF comm. check."

He said it again, and again, six times in total. There was no response, neither voice nor data, from *Columbia.*

Besides the fact that it was out of communication, *Columbia* hadn't shown up on the radar screens. At 9:05 A.M., eleven minutes before the scheduled landing, CNN went live with the first television report of trouble with the shuttle. Controllers went ahead with their routines, but as 9:16, the scheduled landing time, neared, there was no sign of the ship. After another silence, Cain gave instructions to start saving all data for what appeared would soon be necessary—an accident investigation.

He told staff not to make phone calls but was told certain "black" phones could not be shut down. He said he understood, and continued: "Lock the doors." He instructed flight controllers to save all of their notes for the investigation that would certainly follow.

Most of those waiting at Kennedy Space Center's Shuttle Landing Facility realized something was wrong when they didn't hear the twin sonic booms usually heard several minutes before a shuttle lands. A few weren't aware something was wrong until the planned landing time came and went. At least one person speculated the clock might be incorrect.

The shuttle was at an altitude of about 203,000 feet over north-central Texas, traveling at 12,500 miles per hour—18 times the speed of sound—when people who lived below the ship's flight path began sensing something had gone wrong. In later days, eyewitnesses and video footage would indicate problems even as the ship was over California. The first reports, however, came from Texas. A television station in Dallas, Texas, shot video footage of the shuttle as it broke up across the Texas skies. A bright light was seen, followed by smoke plumes streaking diagonally through the sky. Pieces appeared to break off the spacecraft and separate into balls of light as it plummeted earthward.

Debris started falling over several eastern Texas cities, including Palestine and Texarkana. There were no reports of injuries on the ground. But in Nacogdoches, residents found bits of metal strewn across the city. Dentist Jeff Hancock said a metal bracket about a foot long crashed through his office roof. "I could see two bright objects flying off each side of it," said Gary Hunziker of Plano, Texas. "I just assumed they were chase jets." Benjamin Laster of Kemp, Texas, said his barn started shaking. "We ran out and started looking around," he said. "I saw a puff of vapor and smoke and saw big chunks of material fall."

Within minutes, NASA began sending search teams to the Dallas-Fort Worth area. Officials warned people on the ground to stay away from any fallen shuttle debris. Environmental Protection Agency spokesman Joe Martyak said he did not know what toxic chemicals could be amid the debris, because the shuttle can undergo reactions from the intense heat of reentry.

Other news media soon caught up with CNN. "NASA loses communication with space shuttle *Columbia* as the ship soared over Texas several minutes before landing Saturday morning," read an MSNBC e-mail bulletin sent at 9:21 A.M., five minutes after *Columbia* was supposed to have landed. Then CNN.com added, "NASA reports losing contact with space shuttle *Columbia* at 9 A.M. prior to its scheduled landing at 9:16."

A *Jerusalem Post* e-mail bulletin provided a follow-up minutes later: "Space shuttle *Columbia* has broken up on reentry over Texas. No word yet on cause of disaster. NASA has declared emergency situation." A second e-mail bulletin from the *Post* a few minutes later told the rest of the story: "The space shuttle *Columbia* has broken up on reentry and is now descending in four or five pieces over Texas, USA."

Initially, the astronauts' families and guests knew nothing of what was happening. They had gathered in a special area near the landing site at Kennedy Space Center in Florida and were anxiously awaiting the return of their loved ones. "The clock ticked, and we counted, and it was quiet when we should have heard a noise," Rona

Ramon said afterwards. "They took us from there and told us that they didn't know anything, but we knew." Five-year-old Noa, who had uttered her eerie premonition when the shuttle lifted off, then asked: "How can you die in space? People are supposed to die only on earth."

Dr. Yael Barr, of the Israeli Aerospace Medicine Institute, who was waiting at the landing strip for the astronauts' return, said the countdown clock reached zero and began counting upwards. "They were still not there," she said. "I told my friend, 'I have a bad feeling. I think they are gone.' And I was in tears."

Former astronaut John Glenn and his wife were watching television at their home in Maryland. "Any time you lose contact like that, there's some big problem," Glenn said. "Of course, once you went for several minutes without any contact, you knew something was terribly wrong."

Ilan's brother Gadi had gathered relatives and friends in Israel to raise a toast in honor of the landing. Instead, they tried to comfort one another while contemplating his sad fate. "We are in shock and don't know what to do," Gadi Ramon told Israel's Channel 10 television, choking back tears. "This was a dream come true for Ilan. He wrote me e-mails from the shuttle . . . and was literally on cloud nine."

Israelis stopped in their tracks to watch the news. One group that had gathered to play tennis in Tel Aviv crowded around television monitors in disbelief. "It was a celebration for the country and it is ending so tragically," Hezi Yitzhaki said. "An entire country was so proud of him. We are already in such a bad state." Ilan's brother-in-law, Gabi Bar, sobbed as he spoke to a television station a short while later. "This is a moment of crisis," he said. "I don't know how we can come to terms with the loss of Ilan." Ilan's father, Eliezer Wolferman, who was at an Israeli television station to watch the landing, left in shock. He silently boarded a taxi and rode home to Omer, south of Beersheva.

The astronauts' families were taken back to Houston in separate planes. A psychologist and a NASA representative were assigned to each family, but the Ramon family's strongest source of solace was Canadian astronaut Steve MacLean. MacLean, who went into orbit on board *Columbia* 11 years earlier, helped Ilan throughout his training at NASA. MacLean and his wife became close friends of the Ramons, and they were with Rona and the four children after the disaster.

Two hours after the shuttle had been scheduled to land, the giant screen at the front of mission control showed a map of the southwestern United States and what should have been *Columbia*'s flight path. The U.S. flag next to the countdown clock at Kennedy Space Center was lowered to half-staff.

"A contingency for the space shuttle has been declared," mission control somberly repeated over and over.

NASA administrator Sean O'Keefe met with the astronauts' families. Six of the seven astronauts were married, and five had children. When he emerged, O'Keefe, his voice breaking at times, said President Bush had talked to the families of the astronauts. Soon after, the president televised a somber address:

"My fellow Americans, this day has brought terrible news and great sadness to our country. At 9 A.M. this morning, mission control in Houston lost contact with our space shuttle *Columbia*. A short time later, debris was seen falling from the skies above Texas. The *Columbia* is lost; there are no survivors.

"On board was a crew of seven: Colonel Rick Husband, Lieutenant-Colonel Michael Anderson, Commander Laurel Clark, Captain David Brown, Commander William McCool, Dr. Kalpana Chawla, and Ilan Ramon, a colonel in the Israeli Air Force. These men and women assumed great risk in the service to all humanity.

"In an age when space flight has come to seem almost routine, it is easy to overlook the dangers of travel by rocket and the difficulties of navigating the fierce outer atmosphere of the earth. These astronauts knew the dangers, and they faced them willingly, knowing they had a high and noble purpose in life. Because of their courage and daring and idealism, we will miss them all the more.

"All Americans today are thinking, as well, of the families of these men and women who have been given this sudden shock and grief. You're not alone. Our entire nation grieves with you. And those you loved will always have the respect and gratitude of this country.

"The cause in which they died will continue. Mankind is led into the darkness beyond our world by the inspiration of discovery and the longing to understand. Our journey into space will go on.

"In the skies today we saw destruction and tragedy. Yet farther than we can see there is comfort and hope. In the words of the prophet Isaiah, 'Lift your eyes and look to the heavens. Who created all these? He who brings out the starry hosts one by one and calls them each by name. Because of His great power and mighty strength, not one of them is missing.'

"The same creator who names the stars also knows the names of the seven souls we mourn today. The crew of the shuttle *Columbia* did not return safely to Earth; yet we can pray that all are safely home. May God bless the grieving families, and may God continue to bless America."

The Aftermath

NASA administrator Sean O'Keefe continued the early eulogies for the *Columbia* seven hours after the disaster. "This is indeed a tragic day for the NASA family, for the families of the astronauts who flew on STS-107, and likewise it is tragic for the nation," he said. In his statement, O'Keefe added details that were both reassuring and chilling. He said NASA had already begun to investigate the accident by appointing an independent board. (The Congress set up its own investigation.) He also said there was no indication that terrorism had caused the accident. Then he returned to the personal tragedy.

"I was here this morning with the families of the astronauts and their friends. . . . It started out as a pretty happy morning, as we awaited the landing of STS-107. We had highly anticipated their return because we couldn't wait to congratulate them for their extraordinary performance and their excellent effort on this very important science mission. They dedicated their lives to pushing scientific challenges for all of us here on Earth. They dedicated themselves to that objective and did it with a happy heart, willingly, and with great enthusiasm.

"The loss of this valued crew is something we will never be able to get over. We have assured the families that we will do everything, everything we can possibly do, to guarantee that we work our way through this horrific tragedy. We trust the prayers of the nation will be with them and with their families. A more courageous group of people you could not have hoped to know—an extraordinary group of astronauts who gave their lives—and the families of these crew members. They knew exactly the risks. And never, ever, did we want to see a circumstance in which this could happen."

Word of the disaster spread quickly in Israel and the U.S. Jewish community. There was widespread sobbing in the Houston synagogue near the Ramon residence, which conducted an impromptu memorial service for him. Friends, who only three weeks ago bid him farewell and dedicated a book with good luck offerings to him, gathered to mourn his death. Outside Johnson Space Center in Houston, where the astronauts had trained, a makeshift memorial sprung up. Hundreds of people left flowers and handwritten notes.

Vigils were held in front of the U.S. mission to the United Nations and the Israeli consulate. Mourners recalled the pride they felt watching an Israeli orbit the earth.

The other six astronauts were likewise remembered as heroes.

"These great people are not fallen heroes; they gave their lives climbing," said Rabbi Avi Weiss, president of the Coalition for Jewish Concerns, who organized the vigils. Inside the consulate, and at the embassy in Washington and other consulates throughout the United States, mourners were invited to sign commemorative books to honor the fallen astronauts, an honor that is usually reserved for heads of state. "I'm really at a loss for words to express how profoundly I feel about the tragedy and how profoundly I feel for the surviving relatives of the astronauts," said Isaiah Gross, who participated in the vigil.

Leaders of Jewish groups said they were devastated at Ilan's death and noted that events commemorating his achievements were being planned. "He was a person who healed Israel at a time when it so badly needed someone to bring people together," said Malcolm Hoenlein, executive vice chairman of the Conference of Presidents of Major American Jewish Organizations. "Throughout the community there is a profound sense of loss for all the astronauts. Each one of them was a hero, all people who were really true role models." The United Jewish Communities organization released a statement saying that Ramon's participation in the space mission "was testament to the strong and unbreakable ties between our countrymen, and the dedication of the United States and Israel to humankind's constant reach for knowledge, hope, and peace."

Israeli Air Force Commander Major-General Dan Halutz mourned the loss of "a friend, an officer, and a fighter." He also lamented the loss of Ilan's six crewmates. Flags at Israeli Air Force facilities were lowered that night to half-mast. Halutz and others said the loss of the shuttle and an Israeli hero would not mean the end of Israel's forays into space. "I foresee another Israeli astronaut, and I think we should wait and learn what happened," he said. Israel's Education Ministry declared a week of special classes dedicated to Ilan's memory. Palestinian Information Minister Yasser Abed Rabbo said that the Palestinian Authority was "shocked at the news of the tragedy. We sympathize with the families of the astronauts."

The next day, a Hebrew love song, based on a poem attributed to the biblical Rachel and chosen by Ilan Ramon's wife for NASA to broadcast as a wake-up call to him in space, was repeatedly played on Israel radio and TV stations. "Will you hear my voice, my distant one? Will you hear my voice, wherever you are? My last day is perhaps here. The day of parting tears is near." Ilan's wife never explained why she chose the tragically prophetic tune. But on that day, it seemed the entire country wept at the sound of its sad melody.

In Israel, the entire country had something to say the next day when people woke up and realized the accident reported so extensively the night before wasn't a dream or a mistake. With Ilan's death, Israel had lost a national symbol, said Chief Rabbi Yisrael Lau. "He was a proud representative of Judaism and of the land of Israel. He instilled national pride." Lau said people felt a further loss because Ilan's mother was a survivor of Auschwitz. "There was a feeling that he had risen from the ashes."

Editorial, *The Jerusalem Post*, February 2, 2003

Tragedy in Space

"I know my flight is very symbolic for the people of Israel, especially the survivors, the Holocaust survivors, because I was born in Israel, many people will see this as a dream that is come true. I'm kind of the proof for my parents and their generation that whatever we've been fighting for in the last century is becoming true."
—Col. Ilan Ramon, Israel's first astronaut.

It was with those noble sentiments in mind that Ilan Ramon blasted off into space last month, proudly representing his people and his country as a member of the crew of the space shuttle *Columbia*. His valor in life, as well as his personal family history, moved nearly every Israeli, just as his untimely death yesterday during *Columbia*'s reentry shocked and saddened the entire nation.

Even for a country buffeted by death and violence over the past two years, Ramon's death came as an enormous blow. At one time or another, every child looks skyward and imagines what it would be like to venture among the stars. Ramon embodied the fulfillment of those dreams for each and every one of us, lifting our spirits at a time of great national difficulty, and reminding us all of just how far this country has come since its establishment. After all, it was just six decades ago that Ramon's mother and grandmother emerged from the horrors of the Holocaust. As Ramon himself pointed out, it was no less than a "miracle" that he was being sent to represent the sovereign Jewish state as its first astronaut.

Aware of the deep significance of his mission, Ramon sought to underline the importance of Jewish unity and mutual respect. He took aboard various items, such as a kiddush cup, a Book of Psalms and a picture drawn by a 14-year-old Jewish boy named Petr Ginz who was murdered in Auschwitz in 1944. He did this, he said, to 'emphasize the unity of the people of Israel and the Jewish communities abroad.' Though not religiously observant, Ramon also insisted on taking a mezuza along with him, and even asked NASA to supply him with kosher food. 'This is symbolic,' he said. 'I thought it would be nice to represent all kinds of Jews, including religious ones.'

The reasons behind *Columbia*'s disintegration remain unclear, and the investigation into the disaster is likely to take some time. Yesterday's tragedy was the first of its kind in the 42-year history of the US manned space program, which had never before seen an accident during a descent to Earth or landing. It was the 113th flight in NASA's 22-year old shuttle program, and the 28th flight for the *Columbia*, the oldest shuttle.

Yesterday's disaster was equal in its devastation only to the January 28, 1986 explosion of the space shuttle *Challenger* moments after liftoff. In addition to Ramon, there were six other brave men and women on board the shuttle. Indeed, the make-up of *Columbia*'s crew was testimony to the greatness of America, for it included an immigrant from India, a black physicist, and a female flight surgeon, demonstrating yet again that color and gender do not serve as barriers to success in the land of freedom. And, by inviting foreign nationals such as Ramon to fly aboard the shuttle and benefit from American know-how, the U.S. was underlining both its generosity of spirit and benevolence.

In the final analysis, Col. Ramon is likely to be recalled largely for the traumatic circumstances of his death, but that would not be doing justice to the greatness of his life. He fought for his country, defending it in the 1973 Yom Kippur War and the 1982 Lebanon war, and participated in the 1981 bombing of the Iraqi nuclear reactor at Osirak. As Israel's first astronaut, he used his fame to spread a message of inter-Jewish conciliation and unity, reciting the Shema Yisrael prayer as the shuttle flew over Jerusalem. By going into space, Ramon proved how high man can reach when he puts his intellect to productive use. But by reminding us all just how proud we should be of this country and of our identity as Jews, he also showed how high man can soar when his life is devoted to the common good. May Col. Ilan Ramon's memory, and those of his six fellow astronauts, be a blessing.

Prime Minister Sharon invited Daniel Kurtzer, the United States ambassador to Israel, to the following day's Cabinet meeting. He turned to the American diplomat, himself Jewish, and said: "It is at times like these that we feel our common fate, identity and values, and shared vision. The seven astronauts who perished yesterday in the space shuttle *Columbia* disaster are part of the heavy price that the human race must pay in its quest for knowledge and in its desire to explore other worlds. Their deaths will not be in vain. Mankind's journey into space will continue. U.S.-Israeli cooperation in this endeavor will continue as well. The day will come when other Israeli astronauts will be launched into space. I am certain that the memory of Ilan Ramon, Israel's first space pioneer, will be etched in our hearts."

Sharon said he regretted not having known Ilan personally, but added that he was familiar with his record as a "daring fighter pilot" and an excellent officer. "I spoke with Ilan before he lifted off on his last mission, and I also spoke with him during the flight," Sharon continued. "In my conversations with Ilan, I became acquainted with a man of values, who deeply loved this people and this land, a man who should not have been taken from us so suddenly, along with the hopes, dreams, history, and future of all of us to a place higher than we can realize. All Israelis bow their heads in memory of Colonel Ilan Ramon and the crew of the shuttle *Columbia*, heroes of our journey into space." Sharon offered condolences to President Bush, the families of the other astronauts, and the American people.

Kurtzer replied that Israelis and Americans "turned their eyes toward the heavens with pride and anticipation" when the space shuttle had lifted off seventeen days previously. "Our two nations shared joy and admiration for the heroism and bravery of the crew. We shared hopes and dreams of the advances that this mission promised for the betterment of humankind," he said. "Now, Americans and Israelis come together again to mourn. In paying tribute to these heroes, our two nations can draw on deep reservoirs of courage, character, and fortitude. As we share triumph, we also share misfortune."

Kurtzer quoted from what Ilan had said while in space: "The world looks marvelous from up here, so peaceful, so wonderful, and so fragile." His words evoked thoughts of an American poet who said after an earlier *Apollo* flight, "To see the earth as we see it now, small and beautiful and blue in that eternal silence where it floats, is to see ourselves as riders on the earth together; brothers on that bright loveliness in the unending night; brothers who see now that they are truly brothers." Americans and Israelis, Kurtzer said, "are brothers indeed on earth and in space."

Ilan, serious and unassuming, had captured the hearts of his countrymen, and the Israeli media reflected this feeling. "This country, so used to looking down on itself, raised its eyes towards the surprising possibility that after all there is a different Israel, a country that can defy the gravity of its fate," wrote one commentator in the Israeli newspaper *Ha'aretz*. This daily, which only a week before had run a disparaging article about the flight, had changed its tune. "It would be wrong to conclude that, in order to avoid such disasters, space travel should be halted altogether. The death of the first Israeli astronaut, Colonel Ilan Ramon, must not terminate Israel's involvement in the space program," the newspaper wrote.

Yediot Aharonot columnist Eitan Haber lamented that Israel had had few moments of happiness and pride recently. "And we so wanted to be so—happy and proud," he wrote. "We sat down to see the routine landing, and even this unique moment was robbed from us; instead of a smile, and an Israeli flag, and the first homemade astronaut, we saw trails of white vapor in the sky, and it seems an entire state lost a family member." The religious daily newspaper *Hatzofeh* said the disaster, once again, united Israel and the United States. "The sense of a common fate, which became stronger with the upsurge in terrorism and the preparations for war in Iraq, has again found expression in tragedy," it said.

At the entrance to ORT Kiryat Motzkin High School, north of Haifa, students assembled black memorial boards covered with pictures and newspaper clippings of *Columbia* and its crew, as well as pictures of Ilan and the crystal experiment he had performed for them in space. The school was one of six around the world to have an experiment carried out on the mission. Several pupils brought candles that they lit for each of the seven astronauts. Dor Zafrir, 16, said that he and four friends were told to wait for a call from mission control in Houston one night at 2 A.M. When they picked up the phone, mission control informed them that visual and audio connections with *Columbia* were good, and Ilan was going to report on the experiment. The pictures and data sent back showed one crystal growing like a ball and the other growing in all directions—"like spaghetti," one student said. They saw *Columbia* go down, but refused to believe it. "I thought it was someone's joke," Adar Moritz, 17, said. Only on Sunday morning did he realize the astronauts were dead.

Israeli Defense Minister Shaul Mofaz joined air force and space program officials in expressing grief over the news of *Columbia*'s demise. "Ilan was a brave pilot and that is how we will remember him. He had a vision when he became an astronaut, and we will continue that vision," he said the day after the accident at a dedication ceremony for the Forest of the Fallen near Jerusalem in memory of Israel's war dead. Mofaz said the fallen astronaut represented the State of Israel and the whole Jewish people. "We saw Ilan put on the blue-and-white badge that represents us all," he said. "He bore our national symbols and flag with pride and achieved something that few have done before. We will never forget that white stripe that scarred the heavens while below, on earth, everyone was preparing to celebrate his return."

Late on Sunday, about thirty-six hours after the disaster, Rona Ramon appeared before a crowd of reporters in front of her Houston home. She wore dark sunglasses and a shirt with a NASA patch. She began to cry as she told reporters the family had received e-mails from Ilan the day before he was due to land and that he had meant for the whole family to read them together. She said he was with people he loved, in a place that he loved, when he died. "We are one big family," she said of the families of *Columbia*'s crew. "What unites us is the knowledge they really enjoyed being there and loved being with each other. They are all angels and will remain that way." The four Ramon children were quiet and had been unable to express their feelings, Rona explained. "They are trying to get used to the fact that he is no longer here."

Rona said that her husband enjoyed every minute of his mission in space. "He was a true optimist. He didn't even write a will," she said. "It seemed unnecessary to him. But we will carry on his will for life. He had a smile, and we will carry on with that smile."

Brig.-Gen. Raanan Falk, Israeli Air Force attaché in Washington, was with the Ramon family when they returned to Houston. Rona showed him Ilan's last e-mail message from space in which he said how much he missed his family and in which he wrote, "I'll see you soon on the ground." Noa, the youngest child, told Falk: "Daddy is watching us from above. He is staying there."

The families of the *Columbia* Seven released a joint statement:

"On January sixteenth, we saw our loved ones launch into a brilliant, cloud-free sky. Their hearts were full of enthusiasm, pride in country, faith in their God, and a willingness to accept risk in the pursuit of knowledge—knowledge that might improve the quality of life for all mankind. *Columbia*'s sixteen-day mission of scientific discovery was a great success, cut short by mere minutes, yet it will live on forever in our memories. We want to thank the NASA family and people from around the world for their incredible outpouring of love and support. Although we grieve deeply, as do the families of *Apollo* I and *Challenger* before us, the bold exploration of space must go on. Once the root cause of this tragedy is found and corrected, the legacy of *Columbia* must carry on—for the benefit of our children and yours."

In the following days, memorial services were held in Florida, Houston, and Washington. President Bush spoke again, as did rabbis, chaplains, and astronauts who knew the crew of the *Columbia* personally or were touched by them. In

Houston, the night before NASA's official ceremony with the president, Ilan was remembered in a ceremony at Beth Yeshurun, a Houston synagogue. At the memorial, Ilan's father, Eliezer Wolferman, told the two thousand people who attended how grateful he was to the American people, Israel, and NASA for their support. "They really are doing their best," he said.

Daniel Ayalon, the Israeli ambassador to the United States, spoke of how Ilan embodied the triumph of human spirit over tragedy. "It really represents the real nature of Ilan Ramon," Ayalon said. "Ilan Ramon is a national hero. He had a very strong identity as a Jew, as an Israeli. I think his personal story embodies the true triumph of the Jewish people." Rabbi Roy Walter read a passage from Deuteronomy 4:33, in which Moses reminds the Jews of their experience at Sinai. He said Ilan had wanted to recite it on the Sabbath. "I think you will find the words quite chilling," Walter told the gathering. The passage ended, "Did ever a people hear the voice of God speaking out of a fire, as you have, and live?"

The official U.S. government memorial took place on February 4, in Houston. Shortly before the service, President Bush met with the astronauts' families privately to express his condolences. During the forty-five-minute ceremony, Noa Ramon snuggled on her mother's lap. Beside Rona sat her three sons, Assaf, David, and Tal. Wolferman was next to them, with a pin of an interwoven Israeli and U.S. flag on his lapel. To open the ceremony, navy chaplain Rabbi Harold Robinson quoted at length in both Hebrew and English from the poem "After My Death," by Israeli laureate Haim Nahman Bialik: "Before his time did this man depart/ And the song of his life in its midst was stilled."

More prayers and songs followed his remarks. At one point, President Bush shared his handkerchief with the tearful wife and son of Commander Rick Husband, as they sat at the president's side. Then he spoke.

"Their mission was almost complete, and we lost them so close to home," Bush said. "The men and women of the *Columbia* had journeyed more than six million miles and were minutes away from arrival and reunion. The loss was sudden and terrible, and for their families, the grief is heavy. Our nation shares in your sorrow and in your pride. And today we remember not only one moment of tragedy, but seven lives of great purpose and achievement. To leave behind earth and air and gravity is an ancient dream of humanity. For these seven, it was a dream fulfilled. Each of these astronauts had the daring and discipline required of their calling. Each of them knew that great endeavors are inseparable from great risks. And each of them accepted those risks willingly, even joyfully, in the cause of discovery."

He then spoke about each of the seven crew members individually. In speaking about Ilan, he quoted from an e-mail Ilan had sent from space: "The quiet that envelops space makes the beauty even more powerful. And I only hope that the quiet can one day spread to my country."

The president continued with his main theme.

"Our whole nation was blessed to have such men and women serving in our space program," he said. "Their loss is deeply felt, especially in this place, where so many of you called them friends. The people of NASA are being tested once again. In your grief, you are responding as your friends would have wished—with focus, professionalism, and unbroken faith in the mission of this agency. America's space program will go on. This cause of exploration and discovery is not an option we choose; it is a desire written in the human heart. We are that part of creation which seeks to understand all creation. We find the best among us, send them forth into unmapped darkness, and pray they will return. They go in peace for all mankind, and all mankind is in their debt.

"Yet, some explorers do not return. And the loss settles unfairly on a few. The families here today shared in the courage of those they loved. But now they must face life and grief without them. The sorrow is lonely; but you are not alone. In time, you will find comfort and the grace to see you through. And in God's own time, we can pray that the day of your reunion will come. And to the children who miss your mom or dad so much today, you need to know, they love you, and that love will always be with you. They were proud of you. And you can be proud of them for the rest of your life. The final days of their own lives were spent looking down upon this earth. And now, on every continent, in every land they could see, the names of these astronauts are known and remembered. They will always have an honored place in the memory of this country. And today I offer the respect and gratitude of the people of the United States. May God bless you all."

Chief Astronaut Kent Rominger, a friend, office mate, and boss of the *Columbia* Seven, told anecdotes about the crew that brought tears and smiles to the faces of their families and friends. "The world lost seven heroes; we lost seven family members," he said. "But remembering the unique qualities of each and sharing our special memories will help us heal. Every shuttle crew forms a family as they go through the months, and in this case, years of training. But the STS-107 crew grew particularly close."

Rominger described Ilan as a "perfectly poised fighter pilot, with a sparkle in his eyes. His instructors remember a moment, prior to getting in his launch suit, where, standing in thermal underwear and a Santa Claus cap, he quipped, 'Life is not a rehearsal.' He was also extremely caring. From orbit he sent an e-mail encouraging management to immediately reassign this crew, that he could not imagine being part of or flying with any crew that was more deserving or more talented or more capable."

More than ten thousand people attended the memorial, including congressmen and senators, as well as legendary astronauts Neil Armstrong and John Glenn. Outside Johnson Space Center, flowers and balloons from sympathizers accumulated. Aboard the International Space Station, astronauts Ken Bowersox, Don Pettit, and Nikolai Budarin listened to the ceremony and rang their own bell seven times to commemorate their fellow space travelers. At the Israeli embassy in Washington, people came in a steady stream to sign a book of condolences that was delivered to the Ramon family.

Later, four members of Israel's volunteer organization ZAKA (a Hebrew acronym for Disaster Victims' Identification) arrived in Houston to help recover and identify the remains of the seven astronauts. Yisrael Stefanski, an Israeli ZAKA volunteer who happened to be in the United States that week, went with the team to the recovery area around Nacogdoches, Texas. He spoke of how he and the other volunteers had been at the site of many terror attacks in Israel. "Unfortunately, we have too much experience with this type of work," Stefanski said.

In Florida, Rabbi Zvi Konikov of the Chabad Jewish Community Center of the Space Coast in Satellite Beach spoke at that community's memorial. "Last week I was honored to have been a friend of Ilan Ramon, and today I am humbled to be part of his legacy," he said. "As I think of my friend Ilan, I recall the words of King David in the Book of Samuel when told of the loss of his dear friend Jonathan, 'I am pained and distressed over you, my brother Ilan; you were so pleasant to me.'

"For while *Columbia* is gone, our holy mission continues. *Columbia* is gone, yet the astronauts' souls are with God praying for the well being of their families and for all of us. *Columbia* is gone, yet the astronauts' legacy lives on. They wished to serve and they did."

Saying Goodbye

Nine days after the accident, Ilan's coffin, draped by an Israeli flag, was carried by eight air force colonels into a hangar at the IAF base near Israel's Ben-Gurion Airport. The day was ending, and rain drummed on the hangar's roof. A melancholy adaptation of the love song Rona Ramon had arranged for her husband's wake-up call opened the solemn ceremony. Nestled in her mother's arms, as she had been the week before at the official U.S. memorial, Noa Ramon listened to her father's former commander play the tune on the saxophone as he stood by Ilan's flag-draped coffin. Rona and Assaf—the latter wearing one of his father's blue NASA flight jackets with a Star of David arm patch—reached out to touch the coffin. They read, she in Hebrew, and he in English, an e-mail written by Ilan's crewmate, David Brown, to the Ramon family from aboard the *Columbia*. Brown spoke of how moved he was when he read a letter Ilan had carried on the mission from a Holocaust survivor whose seven-year-old daughter had been killed by the Nazis. "I was stunned that such a beautiful planet could harbor such awful things," Assaf read.

A solemn crowd that included former presidents and prime ministers, rabbis, high-school students, and soldiers surrounded the family in the hangar. Prime Minister Ariel Sharon remarked how a memorial service was not how Israel had imagined Ilan's homecoming. "Far up there, at the edge of the scope of human achievement, we could not have had a better and more fitting representative . . . among the best of our sons and warriors," Sharon said. "Ilan, the son of a mother who survived the Holocaust and a father who is a veteran of the War of Independence, was a courageous combat pilot and an outstanding officer, and was among the best of our sons and warriors. On his last mission he soared higher than any other Israeli and realized his dream."

Turning to the family, he said, "The pain you suffer is the pain we all suffer. Ilan has touched the hidden spot in every Jew's heart. His youthful face, his eternal smile, his fresh countenance, the twinkle in his eyes, penetrated our souls. His image, projected from above, was the reflection of Israel at its best, Israel as we would have liked to see it, the Israel we love."

Sharon said Ilan also symbolized the deep connection between Israel and the United States.

"The Star of David, the blue-and-white of our flag, was interwoven with the American stars and stripes, and the common fate of the team poignantly strengthened the staunch partnership between our nations. A day will come when other Israelis will be launched into space in the service of science and progress. For them and for us, Ilan Ramon will always be a source of inspiration as Israel's space pioneer."

Israeli President Moshe Katsav referred to an e-mail Ilan had written to him from space in which he described how, upon seeing Jerusalem from the shuttle, he spontaneously recited the *Shema Yisrael* prayer. The e-mail continued: "I believe, as I said a few times earlier, that we have in Israel the best people with phenomenal abilities, and it takes only the right leadership to lead the people of Israel to reach the sky! Mr. President . . . please convey my deep appreciation to all Israel's citizens, and let them know that I am honored to be their first representative ever in space. In our mission, we have a variety of international scientific experiments and scientists working . . . for the benefit of all mankind. From space our world looks as one unit without borders. So let me call from up here in space: Let's work our way for peace and a better life for every one on Earth."

Katsav said Ilan had become an international Jewish hero, not just because he participated in the shuttle mission, but because of the symbolism he brought to the mission. He honored the Jewish heritage by bringing objects of historical and religious significance into space. Katsav spoke of Ilan as a unifying force. "Here one person was able in his final days, in his short life, from the strength of his personality, to unite all the different parts of the Jewish people."

The pilots carried the coffin back into the rain and into a waiting military vehicle. The family followed, with Rona Ramon holding her daughter's hand. Among the mourners was Indian ambassador Raminder S. Jassal, who said he was glad to be at the ceremony in solidarity with Israel's grief, as one of the American astronauts, Kalpana Chawla, was a native of India. American astronaut Garret Reisman, who is Jewish and knew Ilan, was one of seven astronauts who attended the ceremony.

"I remember Ilan as a confident optimist," Reisman said. "He never had any doubts, he understood the delays. It never troubled him. He would say, 'It's OK.' And I have a feeling that he would say the same thing now if he were able to. He would say, 'It's something that happened, life will go on, other Israelis will fly, other people will fly in space and the work will continue.' That's the kind of guy he was. I would go to talk with him about Israeli events. At the time he was with us there were many momentous events that happened in Israel, and I would be angry about some of the tragedies, and I would talk to Ilan and he would comfort me." Reisman said he last saw Ilan a week before the mission, just as the crew was entering quarantine. "I wished him a good flight. He said, 'Thank you,' and that was it."

The next day, Ilan was laid to rest at a private military ceremony at Moshav Nahalal, a farming community in northern Israel. About two hundred family members, close friends, and comrades-in-arms, including former president and IAF Commander Ezer Weizman, attended the burial on a hillside overlooking Ilan's favorite landscape, where some of the giants in Israeli history, including war hero Moshe Dayan, are buried.

John Lennon's "Imagine," one of the astronauts' wake-up calls, was played as his funeral dirge. The mourners listened to the recording sent to the astronauts, which ended with Ilan's voice translating Lennon's words into Hebrew: "You may say I'm a dreamer, but I'm not the only one."

An honor guard fired three rounds that reverberated through the Galilee hills, signifying the end of the funeral; a policeman at a roadblock bowed his head in respect. Moments later, the IAF saluted its fallen fighter pilot with a flyover of four F-16s above the burial site. As the planes approached the cemetery, one of them veered toward space in the symbolic "missing man" formation.

Ilan Ramon was home.

After My Death
By Haim Nahman Bialik

After my death, thus shall you mourn me:

There was a man—and see: he is no more!
Before his time did this man depart
And the song of his life in its midst was stilled
And alas! One more tune did he have
And now that tune is forever lost
Forever lost!

And great is the pity! For a harp had he
A living and singing soul
And this poet, whenever he voiced it
The inner secrets of his heart it expressed
All its strings his hand would make sing out.
Yet one hidden chord now is lost with him
Round and round it his fingers would dance
One string in his heart, mute has remained
Mute has remained—to this very day!

And great, oh how great, is the pity!
All its life this string would tremble
Silently quivering, silently trembling
To sound the tune that would set it free
Yearning, thirsting, sorrowing, desiring
As the heart sorrows for what fate has decreed
Though its tune was delayed—every day did it wait
And with unheard whisper begged it to come
Its time came and passed, and it never arrived
It never arrived!

And great, oh, how great is the pain
There was a man—and see: he is no more
And the song of his life in its midst is stilled
One more melody did he have
And now that song is forever lost
Forever lost!

Biographies
of the *Columbia Crew*

Rick Husband

Rick Husband, 45, a colonel in the U.S. Air Force, was a test pilot and veteran of one space flight before *Columbia*. He was commander of STS-107.

Husband received a bachelor of science in mechanical engineering from Texas Tech University in 1980 and a master of science in mechanical engineering from California State University-Fresno in 1990.

As commander, Husband was responsible for the overall conduct of the mission. During the mission, he maneuvered *Columbia* as part of several experiments in the shuttle's payload bay that focused on the earth and sun.

He also was senior member of the "Red Team" and worked with the following experiments: European Research In Space and Terrestrial Osteoporosis (ERISTO); Mediterranean Israeli Dust Experiment (MEIDEX); Osteoporosis Experiment in Orbit (OSTEO); the Physiology and Biochemistry Team (PhAB4) suite of experiments, which included calcium kinetics, latent virus shedding, protein turnover and renal stone risk; and shuttle ozone limb sounding experiment (SOLSE-2).

Selected by NASA in December 1994, Husband served as the pilot of STS-96 in 1999—a ten-day mission during which the crew performed the first docking with the International Space Station. He had logged more than 235 hours in space before STS-107.

At the official government memorial in Houston, President George W. Bush said of Husband: "Rick Husband was a boy of four when he first thought of being an astronaut. As a man, and having become an astronaut, he found it was even more important to love his family and serve his Lord. One of Rick's favorite hymns was, 'How Great Thou Art,' which offers these words of praise: 'I see the stars. I hear the mighty thunder. Thy power throughout the universe displayed.'"

William C. McCool

William C. McCool, 41, a commander in the U.S. Navy, was a former test pilot. He was the pilot of STS-107. He received a bachelor of science in applied science from the U.S. Naval Academy in 1983, a master of science in computer science from the University of Maryland in 1985, and a master of science in aeronautical engineering from the U.S. Naval Postgraduate School in 1992.

McCool, as a member of the "Blue Team," worked with the following experiments: European Space Agency (ESA) Advanced Respiratory Monitoring System (ARMS); ESA Biopack (eight experiments); Mediterranean Israeli Dust Experiment (MEIDEX); and the Physiology and biochemistry team (PhAB4) suite of experiments, which include calcium kinetics, latent virus shedding, protein turnover and renal stone risk.

He was also responsible for maneuvering *Columbia* as part of several experiments mounted in the shuttle's payload bay. Selected by NASA in April 1996, McCool was making his first space flight.

At the official government memorial in Houston, President Bush said of McCool: "The *Columbia*'s pilot was Commander Willie McCool, whom friends knew as the most steady and dependable of men. In Lubbock today they're thinking back to the Eagle Scout who became a distinguished naval officer and a fearless test pilot. One friend remembers Willie this way: 'He was blessed, and we were blessed to know him.'"

Michael P. Anderson

Michael P. Anderson, 43, a lieutenant colonel in the U.S. Air Force, was a former instructor pilot and tactical officer, and a veteran of one previous space flight before STS-107. He was payload commander and mission specialist 3 for STS-107. As payload commander he was responsible for the management of the science mission aboard STS-107.

Anderson received a bachelor of science in physics/astronomy from the University of Washington in 1981 and a master of science in physics from Creighton University in 1990. Anderson, as a member of the "Blue Team," worked with the following experiments: European Space Agency Advanced Respiratory Monitoring System (ARMS); Combustion Module (CM-2), which includes the Laminar Soot Processes (LSP), Water Mist Fire Suppression (MIST) and Structures of Flame Balls at Low Lewis-number (SOFBALL) experiments; Mediterranean Israeli Dust Experiment (MEIDEX); Mechanics of Granular Materials (MGM); and the Physiology and Biochemistry Team (PhAB4) suite of experiments, which include calcium kinetics, latent virus shedding, protein turnover and renal stone risk.

Selected by NASA in December 1994, Anderson flew on STS-89 in 1998—the eighth shuttle-Mir docking mission. Anderson had logged over 211 hours in space before *Columbia*'s flight.

At the official government memorial in Houston, President Bush said of Anderson: "Michael Anderson always wanted to fly planes, and rose to the rank of lieutenant colonel in the air force. Along the way, he became a role model—especially for his two daughters and for the many children he spoke to in schools. He said to them, 'Whatever you want to be in life, you're training for it now.' He also told his minister, 'If this thing doesn't come out right, don't worry about me, I'm just going on higher.'"

David M. Brown

David M. Brown, 46, a captain in the U.S. Navy, was a naval aviator and flight surgeon. He was mission specialist 1 for STS-107. Brown received a bachelor of science in biology from the College of William and Mary in 1978 and a doctorate in medicine from Eastern Virginia Medical School in 1982.

Brown, as a member of the "Blue Team," worked with the following experiments: European Space Agency Advanced Respiratory Monitoring System (ARMS); Combustion Module (CM-2), which included the Laminar Soot Processes (LSP), Water Mist Fire Suppression (MIST) and Structures of Flame Balls at Low Lewis-number (SOFBALL) experiments; Mediterranean Israeli Dust Experiment (MEIDEX); and the Physiology and Biochemistry Team (PhAB4) suite of experiments, which included calcium kinetics, latent virus shedding, protein turnover and renal stone risk.

Selected by NASA in April 1996, Brown was making his first space flight.

At the official government memorial in Houston, President Bush said of Brown: "David Brown was first drawn to the stars as a little boy with a telescope in his back yard. He admired astronauts, but, as he said, 'I thought they were movie stars. I thought I was kind of a normal kid.' David grew up to be a physician, an aviator who could land on the deck of a carrier in the middle of the night, and a shuttle astronaut.

"Brown's brother had asked him several weeks earlier what would happen if something went wrong on their mission. David replied, 'This program will go on.'"

Kalpana Chawla

Kalpana Chawla, 41, was an aerospace engineer and an FAA Certified Flight Instructor. Chawla served as flight engineer and mission specialist 2 for STS-107. She received a bachelor of science in aeronautical engineering from Punjab Engineering College, India, in 1982, a master of science in aerospace engineering from the University of Texas-Arlington in 1984, and a doctorate in aerospace engineering from the University of Colorado-Boulder in 1988.

As a member of the "Red Team," Chawla, with Husband, was responsible for maneuvering *Columbia* as part of several experiments in the shuttle's payload bay. Chawla also worked with the following experiments: Astroculture (AST); Advanced Protein Crystal Facility (APCF); Commercial Protein Crystal Growth (CPCG-PCF); Biotechnology Demonstration System (BDS); ESA Biopack (eight experiments); Combustion Module (CM-2), which includes the Laminar Soot Processes (LSP), Water Mist Fire Suppression (MIST) and Structures of Flame Balls at Low Lewis-number (SOFBALL) experiments; Mechanics of Granular Materials (MGM); Vapor Compression Distillation Flight Experiment (VCD FE); and the Zeolite Crystal Growth Furnace (ZCG).

Selected by NASA in December 1994, Chawla was the prime robotic arm operator on STS-87 in 1997, the fourth U.S. microgravity payload flight. STS-87 focused on how the weightless environment of space affects various physical processes. Chawla had logged more than 376 hours in space before STS-107.

At the official government memorial in Houston, President Bush said of Chawla: "None of our astronauts traveled a longer path to space than Kalpana Chawla. She left India as a student, but she would see the nation of her birth, all of it, from hundreds of miles above. When the sad news reached her hometown, an administrator at her high school recalled, 'She always said she wanted to reach the stars. She went there, and beyond.' Kalpana's native country mourns her today, and so does her adopted land."

Laurel Clark

Laurel Clark, 41, a commander (captain-select) in the U.S. Navy and a naval flight surgeon, was mission specialist 4 on STS-107. Clark received a bachelor of science in zoology from the University of Wisconsin-Madison in 1983 and a doctorate in medicine from the same school in 1987.

Clark, as a member of the "Red Team," worked with the following experiments: European Space Agency (ESA); Advanced Respiratory Monitoring System (ARMS); Astroculture (AST-1 and 2); Biotechnology Demonstration System (BDS); ESA Biopack (eight experiments); Application of Physical and Biological Techniques to Study the Gravisensing and Response System of Plants: Magnetic Field Apparatus (Biotube-MFA); Closed Equilibrated Biological Aquatic System (CEBAS); Commercial ITA Biological Experiments (CIBX); the Microbial Physiology Flight Experiments Team (MPFE) experiments, which included: the effects of microgravity on microbial physiology and spaceflight effects on fungal growth, metabolism and sensitivity to antifungal drugs; osteoporosis experiment in orbit (OSTEO); the physiology and biochemistry team (PhAB4) suite of experiments, which includes calcium kinetics, latent virus shedding, protein turnover and renal stone risk; sleep-wake actigraphy and light exposure during spaceflight (SLEEP); and the vapor compression distillation flight experiment (VCD FE).

Selected by NASA in April 1996, Clark was making her first space flight.

At the official government memorial in Houston, President Bush said of Clark: "Laurel Salton Clark was a physician and a flight surgeon who loved adventure, loved her work, loved her husband and her son. A friend who heard Laurel speaking to mission control said, 'There was a smile in her voice.'

"Laurel conducted some of the experiments as *Columbia* orbited the Earth, and described seeing new life emerge from a tiny cocoon. 'Life,' she said, 'continues in a lot of places, and life is a magical thing.'"